HOOKed
ON KNitting

Hooked on Knitting

20 FRESH AND FUNKY HAND-KNIT DESIGNS

Jessica Biscoe

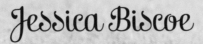

BARRON'S

Photography by Keiko Oikawa

contents

WHAT'S INSIDE...

introduction

As a young child I always had a desire to create. From sketching my pet hamster at age three, to raiding my mum's art cupboard in the summer holidays, I was forever making things… or so I thought. My efforts earned me the nickname "Messy Jessy," so the success of my artistic endeavors is debatable!

Fast forward to 2008, business degree in hand, I was thrown headfirst into the corporate world and soon found myself yearning to create again. The resurgence of the craft movement at this time was a key inspiration, and I felt compelled to equip myself with a traditional skill that would allow me to create something tangible, and useful, with my own hands.

Knitting caught my imagination (thanks to an inspired birthday present), and it's safe to say I quickly became obsessed, devouring every book, blog, tutorial, and article I could find. From the outset I was particularly interested in the design process and different construction techniques; I needed to know how and why, preferring to create my own pieces, rather than follow patterns.

Putting this book together has been a hugely enjoyable experience that has immersed me in those design elements that I love the most. I particularly enjoyed deciding on the best stitch patterns and shaping methods for the Ballerina Slippers and Porcupine Paperweight. I also took pleasure in creating the larger homeware items, such as the Triangle Motif Throw, which has a lovely drape and luxurious texture— perfect for an evening on the sofa with a good book!

I really hope you enjoy making and using these projects as much as I did creating them.

Happy knitting!

Jessica

x

knitting basics

- Knitting kit • Choosing yarns • Deciphering knitting patterns • Working from knitting charts • Starting to knit • Making a slip knot • Casting on • Working the knit stitch • Working the purl stitch • Binding off • Decreasing • Increasing • Measuring gauge • Tips for novice knitters

knitting kit

The most basic knitting kit can consist of nothing more than two needles and a tape measure, but there is a selection of other useful items that are good for a knitter to have in their arsenal.

Knitting needles

Knitting needles come in a variety of lengths and thicknesses, depending on the yarn you are knitting with and how many stitches you want to hold on your needle. The general rule of thumb is that when you knit with really thick yarn you will need to use thicker needles, and when you knit with finer yarn you are likely to use thinner needles. When you buy yarn, the label on the ball, hank, or skein always has a suggested needle size on it recommended by the manufacturer, but you can always play around with this if you want a tighter or looser stitch than the one suggested. You can also get circular needles for knitting in the round. Basically, these are two shorter needles connected by a long nylon wire. You can use circular needles for knitting in rows as well as working in the round, just make sure at the end of each row you swap the needles over in your hands and knit back the way you've just come, rather than continue to knit around and around.

Stitch holders

A few stitch holders are very useful for when knitting garments. Whenever you have stitches that at any point are not being worked—around a neckline on a sweater, for example—then slip these unworked stitches onto a stitch holder in order to hold them securely while you continue with a different section of knitting. These stitches may then be returned later to the needles from the stitch holder once you are ready to work with them again. Safety pins are a good, inexpensive alternative to stitch holders for holding just a small number of stitches.

Cable needles

Cable needles are short open-ended needles—sometimes with a shallow V-shape in the center—which hold a few stitches at a time, mainly used for decorative cables.

Needle gauge

If you have a collection of vintage knitting needles, which can be picked up from thrift stores or yard sales, a gauge is really useful. As the sizing system isn't the same in all countries, this is the best way to confirm the size of any needle.

Row counter

A row counter is a tiny cylinder with rotating numbers that slips onto a knitting needle. Each time you complete a row, change the number so you know where you are in your pattern at all times.

Stitch markers

You don't have to buy purpose-made stitch markers, but I adore my tiny teacup stitch markers. You can use pretty much anything at hand—colored elastic bands, loops of contrasting yarn, or even paper clips—to mark the beginning of rounds when knitting on circular needles, key places in a repeat stitch pattern, or the point of an increase or decrease when shaping.

Yarn needle

Always keep a few blunt-tipped yarn needles—darning or tapestry needles—with an eye that is large enough to thread yarn through for seaming and stitching up knitted garments. It's preferable not to use needles that are too fine, as you often find yourself stitching through the knitted yarn and splitting it. A bodkin, which is similar to a needle but is very thick with a big eye, is perfect for stitching up bulky knitted garments.

Pins and safety pins

Pins and safety pins are always useful for pinning seams together before you stitch them, so you know you're sewing evenly.

Tape measure

A dressmaker's tape measure is crucial for checking your knitted gauge or measuring your knitting.

choosing yarns

There is an amazing array of hand-knit yarns available, in a kaleidoscope of colors and a range of different thicknesses. If you don't like using the recommended yarn for a particular pattern, another yarn of the same thickness may be substituted (see page 126). So, if I recommend using an Aran-weight yarn, you can substitute this for another medium-weight yarn. Just make sure you work a gauge swatch and match the recommended gauge.

Super-fine-weight yarn (sock, fingering, baby)
Average knitted gauge over 4": 27–32 stitches
Recommended needles: US sizes 1–3 (2.25–3.25 mm)

Fine-weight yarn (sport, baby)
Average knitted gauge over 4": 23–26 stitches
Recommended needles: US sizes 3–5 (3.25–3.75 mm)

Lightweight yarn (double knitting, light worsted)
Average knitted gauge over 4": 21–24 stitches
Recommended needles: US sizes 5–7 (3.75–4.5 mm)

You will find a handy knitting needle conversion chart on the inside front flap of this book, listing three standard knitting needle sizes—US sizes, European metric sizes, and old UK and Canadian imperial sizes.

Medium-weight yarn (Aran, worsted, afghan)
Average knitted gauge over 4": 16–20 stitches
Recommended needles: US sizes 7–9
(4.5–5.5 mm)

Bulky-weight yarn (chunky, craft, rug)
Average knitted gauge over 4": 12–15 stitches
Recommended needles: US sizes 9–11 (5.5–8 mm)

Super-bulky-weight yarn (bulky, roving)
Average knitted gauge over 4": 6–11 stitches
Recommended needles: US size 11 (8 mm) and larger

Whatever yarn you choose, the yarn label will provide information on recommended needle sizes, gauge, and the weight and length of the yarn. When buying more than one ball of any yarn, check they all have the same dye-lot number, as there can be subtle color differences between batches, which may show when knitted. While knitting a project, keep a note of the dye-lot number in case you need to buy more yarn.

Deciphering Knitting Patterns

To the beginner, a knitting pattern can look like a string of incomprehensible goobledygook. Each line of a knitting pattern is like a recipe and once you understand the format and have learned the terminology, knitting patterns are a breeze to follow.

A pattern leads you through making an entire piece of knitting. Beginning with the amount of yarn, the size of needles, and number of stitches to cast on, the pattern then continues to outline, row by row, what to do. It takes a while to become familiar with the language of knitting patterns. Here is a list of the abbreviations used in this book for you to familiarize yourself with. There is also a handy list on the inside back flap of the book. Any special abbreviations, such as those for cables, are given with the individual patterns.

Be aware of what parentheses ( ) and brackets [ ] are used for in a pattern. Parentheses are sometimes used around stitch counts (the number of stitches in a row). They also indicate the different stitches or measurements for multiple sizes. The first size is shown outside the parentheses and the remaining sizes within them. Brackets are used for repeating instructions.

ABBREVIATIONS

beg begin(ning)
cont continu(e)(ing)
DK double knitting (a lightweight yarn—see page 12)
foll follow(s)(ing)
g gram(s)
k knit
k2tog knit next 2 stitches together
kfb knit into front and back of next stitch
m meter(s)
M1 make one; insert left needle from front to back under strand between st just worked and next st, and knit it through back loop
M1L make one left; work as M1
M1R make one right; insert left needle from back to front under strand between st just worked and next st, and knit it through front loop
mm millimeter(s)
oz ounce(s)
p purl
p2tog purl next 2 stitches together
patt(s) pattern(s); work in pattern

pm place marker
rem remain(s)(ing)
rep repeat(s)(ing)
RS right side
sl slip; slip stitch from left needle onto right needle without knitting it
sm slip marker
ssk slip next 2 sts knitwise, one at a time, insert left needle into front of these 2 sts and knit them together
st(s) stitch(es)
St st stockinette stitch
tbl through back loop(s)
tog together
WS wrong side
yd yard(s)
yo yarn over top of right-hand needle, from front to back, to make a new stitch

[ ] Work instructions within brackets as many times as directed.

* Work from asterisks or between them as directed.

working from knitting charts

Instead of being written out row by row using standard knitting terminology, a color motif or repeat pattern can be represented as a chart on graph paper. All the colorwork motifs for the projects in this book are given as charts—so that, at a glance, you can see exactly what the finished result should look like.

Colorwork instructions can either be written out in full within the pattern or represented as a chart. The various shades of yarn that make up the colorwork motif or repeat pattern are represented either as a symbol or—more commonly—as a color, specified in a key.

Each square of the chart represents one stitch, and each line of squares represents one row of knitting. With both types of chart the right-side rows (or odd-numbered rows) are read from right to left, while the wrong-side rows (or even-numbered rows) are read from left to right. The rows of the chart are read from the bottom to the top.

For the Triangle Motif Throw on pages 106–109 and the Chevron Pillow on pages 114–117, the color chart shows the 8-stitch pattern repeat that is knitted as many times as instructed across the row.

For both the Cozy Mittens adorned with cute squirrels on pages 54–59 and the fabulous Flamingo Pillow on pages 100–105, the colorwork motifs were embroidered onto the finished knitted piece using duplicate stitch. You will find instructions on how to work duplicate stitch on page 104.

Each square of the chart represents one stitch

KEY FOR CHART

- Bambi
- Rust
- Ecru
- Black

Each colored square in the chart relates to the color yarn given in the key

Each line of squares represents one row of knitting

16

starting to knit

As for many crafts, within knitting there are various different methods you can employ in order to achieve the same end result. Knitting is practiced all around the world and varying techniques have evolved in different regions. There is no right way or wrong way to knit. The best way is the method that you find most comfortable, so when you are first learning to knit try out different hand positions until you hit upon the one that comes most naturally to you.

With the exception of making a slip knot, two methods are demonstrated for each of the basic techniques shown in this section. The first is the method most commonly used in the US and UK, where the working yarn is manipulated with the right hand and which is shown on the left-hand pages in orange yarn. The second is the one more regularly employed in Continental Europe, where the yarn is moved by the left hand and which is pictured on the right-hand pages in gray yarn.

Making a slip knot

The slip knot is the very first stitch you make when starting any piece of knitting. Without the slip knot you won't be able to work a single row, as it acts as the anchor for all knitting, so this is the first technique you need to practice and master. Once you know how, making a slip knot is simple.

1 Make the yarn into a loose figure eight shape, holding the tail end of the yarn in your right hand and the loop of yarn in your left hand.

2 Pass the working yarn from your right hand through the loop in your left hand, ensuring that you keep hold of the tail end of the yarn with your right hand and hold the new loop of yarn with your left hand.

3 Pull this new loop of yarn through the left-hand loop, keeping hold of both the yarn ends in your right hand. This forms a slip knot. Place the slip knot on your knitting needle and pull the ends to tighten the loop. This counts as your first stitch.

casting on

Casting on is the term used for when you make the first row of stitches on your knitting needle. No matter what you are making, the pattern will always start with the instruction to cast on a certain number of stitches. There are countless different ways of casting on, but two of the most common methods—and the ones I use most often—are the knit-on and long-tail cast-on.

1 With the slip knot on the left needle, which counts as the first stitch, insert the right needle tip up into the stitch, crossing the right needle under the left needle.

2 With your right hand, wrap the working end of the yarn—the end attached to the ball—around the right needle in a counterclockwise motion.

3 Catching the working yarn that has just been wound around the needle, bring the right needle tip through the loop on the left needle and to the front of the stitch.

4 Insert the left needle from right to left into the loop on the right needle and slide the right needle out. Pull the yarn to tighten the new loop and complete the second stitch.

5 To make subsequent stitches, insert the right needle tip into the stitch just made on the left needle, make another stitch as before and place it on the left needle.

The long-tail cast-on method is a useful technique to know. The most popular method of casting on used in Continental Europe, this technique gives a firm cast-on edge. It is called the long-tail cast-on, as you need to leave a tail end of yarn long enough to make all the required stitches. Placing the slip knot on two needles prevents the cast-on edge from becoming too tight.

1 Place the slip knot on two needles. Wrap the tail end yarn over your left thumb and the working yarn over your index finger, holding both yarn strands in your palm.

2 Take the needles down and under the loop around your thumb, swooping upward toward the strand over your index finger.

3 Next take the needles up and over the loop around your index finger, swooping downward this time.

4 Draw the yarn wrapped over your index finger caught on the needles through the loop around your thumb to form a stitch.

5 Slip the loop off your thumb and tighten the newly cast-on stitch on the needles. Repeat these steps until you have the required number of stitches.

working the knit stitch

This is the key basic stitch to learn. Most other knitting stitches are a variation on the knit stitch, so this simple four-step process is an important technique to master. The most common technique for working the knit stitch in the US and UK is known as the English method, which is shown on this page. Opposite is an alternative technique called the Continental method. With the English method, your right hand controls the flow and tension of the working yarn, wrapping it around the needle.

1 Holding the needle full of stitches in your left hand, insert the right needle tip up through the first stitch on the left needle so the right needle crosses behind the left.

2 With your right hand, wrap the working yarn in a counterclockwise motion around the back of the right needle and then between the tips of both crossed needles.

3 With the right needle tip, pull the working yarn that has just been wound around through the loop on the left needle.

4 Slide the existing stitch off the left needle, leaving the newly formed stitch on the right needle. Repeat these steps until all the stitches on the left needle have been worked.

The Continental method for working the knit stitch uses a different yarn position than the English method. With this technique, you hold the yarn static in your left hand and move the right needle to catch and pull the strand of yarn through the loop on the left needle to form a new stitch. A lot of knitters find this Continental method to be a quicker way to knit.

1 Holding the needle full of stitches in your left hand, insert the right needle tip up through the first stitch on the left needle so the right needle crosses behind the left.

2 Keeping a firm yarn tension, catch the working yarn with the right needle tip by swooping it under the strand.

3 With the right needle tip, pull the working yarn through the existing stitch. If necessary, hold the strand in place on the needle with your right finger.

4 Slide the existing stitch off the left needle, leaving the newly formed stitch on the right needle. Repeat these steps until all the stitches on the left needle have been worked.

working the purl stitch

The next technique to learn is the purl stitch, which looks exactly like the reverse of a knit stitch. As perfect partners, the knit and purl stitches are used in combination to create endless stitch patterns. Again, the most common technique for working the purl stitch in the US and UK is the English method, which is shown on this page. When knitting the purl stitch the working yarn is held at the front of the work rather than at the back as with the knit stitch. Also, whereas the right needle is inserted into a stitch from left to right when working the knit stitch, with the purl stitch you insert the needle from right to left.

1 With the working yarn at the front, insert the right needle tip up through the first stitch on the left needle so the right needle crosses in front of the left needle.

2 With your right hand, wrap the working yarn in a counterclockwise motion around the right needle and then between the tips of both crossed needles.

3 With the right needle tip, pull the working yarn that has just been wound around through the loop on the left needle.

4 Slide the existing stitch off the left needle, leaving the newly formed stitch on the right needle. Repeat these steps until all the stitches on the left needle have been worked.

To work the purl stitch using the Continental method, you hold the yarn in your left hand just like its knit stitch partner on page 23.

1 Holding the needle full of stitches in your left hand, insert the right needle tip up through the first stitch on the left needle so the right needle crosses in front of the left.

2 Keeping a firm yarn tension, catch the working yarn with the right needle tip by swooping it under the strand.

3 With the right needle tip, pull the working yarn through the existing stitch. If necessary, hold the strand in place on the needle with your right finger.

4 Slide the existing stitch off the left needle, leaving the newly formed stitch on the right needle. Repeat these steps until all the stitches on the left needle have been worked.

Binding Off

When a piece of knitting is finished you need to take it off the needles. So the work does not unravel, the stitches must be bound off. Keep your stitches looser than usual when binding off to stop the bound-off edge from puckering and spoiling your knitting. This page shows how to bind off using the English knitting method.

1 When binding off knitwise, knit two stitches in the usual way. Insert the left needle tip into the front of the first of these two knitted stitches.

2 Carefully lift the first knitted stitch on the right needle over the second and off the right needle.

3 Release the stitch from the left needle tip to leave one stitch on the right needle. Knit one more stitch, then repeat step 2.

4 When you have bound off all the stitches on the left needle and have one stitch left on the right needle, cut the working yarn, leaving a long yarn tail.

5 Loosen the final stitch to make a bigger loop and remove the knitting needle. Pass the cut end of the working yarn through this last loop and tighten the loop to fasten off.

Binding off is done in the same way if you are knitting using the Continental method, except that, as usual, the yarn is held in the left hand instead of the right.

1 When binding off knitwise, knit two stitches in the usual way. Insert the left needle tip into the front of the first of these two knitted stitches.

2 Carefully lift the first knitted stitch on the right needle over the second and off the right needle.

3 Release the stitch from the left needle tip to leave one stitch on the right needle. Knit one more stitch, then repeat step 2.

4 When you have been bound off all the stitches on the left needle and have one stitch left on the right needle, cut the working yarn, leaving a long yarn tail.

5 Loosen the final stitch to make a bigger loop and remove the knitting needle. Pass the cut end of the working yarn through this last loop and tighten the loop to fasten off.

Decreasing knit 2 together

The easiest way to decrease the number of stitches in a row, is to knit two stitches together. This is as simple as it sounds. The abbreviation for this is "k2tog," which just means "knit 2 stitches together." As with most things in knitting, there are several ways to decrease stitches. This is the most straightforward and most commonly used method. Follow this page to learn the technique using the English knitting method or the next page if you are using the Continental method.

1 When placing the right needle tip into the stitches on the left needle, instead of picking up just one stitch, pick up the next two stitches at the same time.

2 Wrap the yarn around the right needle as you would with a normal knit stitch in a counterclockwise motion.

3 Catching the yarn that you've just wound around, bring the right needle tip through both the loops on the left needle.

4 Slide the two stitches off the left needle to make one new stitch on the right needle.

1 When placing the right needle tip into the stitches on the left needle, instead of picking up just one stitch, pick up the next two stitches at the same time.

2 Wrap the yarn around the right needle as you would with a normal knit stitch in a counterclockwise motion.

3 Catching the yarn that you've just wound around, bring the right needle tip through both the loops on the left needle.

4 Slide the two stitches off the left needle to make one new stitch on the right needle.

Decreasing

This is another really simple way to decrease the number of stitches on your needles. It's very similar to k2tog. However instead of inserting the right needle from left to right through the fronts of two stitches, you insert it from right to left through the backs of the two stitches. The abbreviation "k2tog tbl" just means "knit 2 stitches together through the back loops." Follow this page if you knit in the English style or the next page if you knit in the Continental style.

1 Place the right needle tip through the two stitches at the back of the work.

2 Wrap the yarn around the needle, as you would with a normal knit stitch, in a counterclockwise motion.

3 Catching the yarn that you've just looped around, pull the tip of the needle through both of the stitches.

4 Slide both stitches off the left needle leaving just the one new stitch on the right needle.

Abbreviation:
k2tog tbl

1 Place the right needle tip through the two stitches at the back of the work.

2 Wrap the yarn around the needle as you would with a normal knit stitch, in a counterclockwise motion.

3 Catching the yarn that you've just looped around, pull the tip of the needle through both of the stitches.

4 Slide both stitches off the left needle leaving just the one new stitch on the right needle.

increasing knit into front & back

When you increase within a row of knitting you can simply cast on one stitch at the appropriate point. This way of increasing gives a far neater finish and is often used in patterns for garments. With this increase method you knit into the front and back of the same stitch, making two stitches from one stitch. This page is for English-method knitters and the next page is for Continental-method knitters.

1 Insert the needle into the stitch as usual, wrap the yarn around and pull it through, but do not slip the loop off the left needle.

2 Keeping the new stitch on the right needle, insert the needle into the back of the same stitch.

3 Wrap the yarn around the right needle tip, as with any knit stitch.

4 Catch the yarn that has been wrapped around and bring the right needle tip through the stitch.

5 Slide the old stitch off the left needle. You now have two new stitches on the right needle.

1 Insert the needle into the stitch as usual, wrap the yarn around and pull it through, but do not slip the loop off the left needle.

2 Keeping the new stitch on the right needle, insert the needle into the back of the same stitch.

3 Wrap the yarn around the right needle tip as with any knit stitch.

4 Catch the yarn that has been wrapped around and bring the right needle tip through the stitch.

5 Slide the old stitch off the left needle. You now have two new stitches on the right needle.

increasing make one

Within a knitting pattern, when you are instructed to make an increase with the command "M1" this abbreviation means "make one stitch." The method for making this new stitch is the same wherever you are within the row. The result adds one stitch to the row. If you knit with the yarn held in your right hand, follow this page; the next page is for those who hold the yarn in the left hand.

1 With the left needle tip, lift the horizontal bar between the unworked and worked stitches. If the picked up loop is too tight to knit easily, loosen it with your fingers.

2 Insert the right needle tip into this new loop on the left needle through the back of the loop—this twists the loop so a hole does not form under it.

3 Wrap the working yarn around the right needle in the usual way.

4 With the right needle tip, pull the working yarn through the loop on the left needle.

5 Slide the picked up stitch off the left needle. This adds one stitch to the row.

1 With the left needle tip, lift the horizontal bar between the unworked and worked stitches. If the picked up loop is too tight to knit easily, loosen it with your fingers.

2 Insert the right needle tip into this new loop on the left needle through the back of the loop—this twists the loop so a hole does not form under it.

3 Wrap the working yarn around the right needle in the usual way.

4 With the right needle tip, pull the working yarn through the loop on the left needle.

5 Slide the picked up stitch off the left needle. This adds one stitch to the row.

measuring gauge

In the same way that everyone's handwriting is slightly different, so is everyone's knitting. Each knitter works with his/her own yarn tension depending on how they hold and control the yarn—some knitters knit tightly, some knitters knit loosely, while others knit with an average tension.

Working and measuring a gauge swatch before you start to knit any pattern is very important, especially if you are a beginner. The point of it is just to ensure that you are knitting to the same gauge the pattern is written with so you know that your hand knit will come out the right size and as the designer intended it.

If your gauge matches that given at the beginning of the pattern, then your project will knit up to the exact size required. Achieving an exact gauge is especially important when knitting garments; however it is less essential for some of the projects in this book, such as the bracelets on pages 72–75, as they do not need to fit exactly and can be adjusted.

The gauge given at the beginning of a knitting pattern is almost always written giving the number of stitches and rows in a 4" square. It's best if you knit a swatch about 5" square so you can take a measurement from the center of the swatch.

When you have knitted up a gauge square, lay it on a flat surface and, using a tape measure and some pins, mark a 4" square. Count the number of stitches within the pins. Each stitch looks like a "V" and you will find generally that there are more rows (vertically) than stitches (horizontally). This is because knit stitches are wider than they are tall.

Once you have counted the stitches and the rows within this 4" x 4" square, compare your gauge to that given in the pattern. If it matches, that's great, you can begin to knit the pattern. If it doesn't match, don't worry. If you find that you have more stitches within the 4" that the pattern states, this means that you are knitting tightly and should try knitting another gauge swatch using slightly thicker needles. If you find that you have fewer stitches within the 4", then this means that you are knitting loosely and should try knitting another gauge swatch using slightly thinner needles. It may seem painstaking at first, but it's definitely worth getting right.

tips for novice knitters

Knitting is a relaxing hobby, so enjoy the craft. Don't get bogged down trying to instantly master every technique and don't panic if you drop a stitch. Have fun playing around with the endless possibilities of knitting.

PRACTICE HOLDING THE YARN

Wrap the working end of the yarn (the one attached to the ball) once around the index finger of your right hand. Everyone has their own way of holding the yarn, but while you are learning this is the easiest way to keep the yarn in the correct place. It also helps to produce an even gauge when knitting.

WORK A GAUGE SWATCH

It's so important to get into the habit of knitting a gauge swatch. No matter how tempting it is to dive in and begin the pattern, you need to know that you are creating the correct gauge. If your gauge isn't right, you may end up with an ill-fitting garment. Use the gauge swatch for practicing your basic stitches, as well as casting on and binding off. You can always put gauge squares to use afterward by stitching lots together to make a scarf or a throw.

READ THE PATTERN

When starting a knitting project, take the time to read through all the instructions beforehand so you know what to expect. As you work through the pattern, either tick off where you are or keep a row counter handy so you don't forget which part you've already knitted.

FIX ANY MISTAKES

Most mistakes in knitting are easily fixed. Learning to do this will give you confidence and ease the frustration when something doesn't look quite right. Unraveling your knitting should be a last resort—for your sanity more than anything else!

TUTORIAL VIDEOS

When you don't have a knitter friend nearby to help you, watching tutorial videos online can offer quick answers and explanations. You will find a helpful selection on my own website, www.jessicabiscoe.co.uk.

JOIN A KNITTING GROUP

Find a knitting buddy or join a group. When teaching yourself to knit, at times it can be frustrating so it's good to be surrounded by others who can answer questions and offer help. You can learn just by watching other knitters. It's also a good way to meet people, share ideas, and feel inspired by what they are creating.

IMPROVISE

Hair pins and safety pins make fantastic stitch holders and cable needles. And, if you don't have any stitch markers yet, a knotted loop of scrap yarn will do the trick.

STRAIGHT OR ROUND

Circular needles are used to knit in the round but long ones can also be used in place of straight needles to knit large items, like throws, in rows. I have a set of interchangeable circular needles, with different length cables, that I use for all my knitting.

SIGN UP TO RAVELRY
There's a whole world of patterns and helpful, knowledgeable folk waiting for you at www.ravelry.com.

COUNT YOUR STITCHES
Counting your stitches at the end of each row means you'll know immediately when something has gone wrong and you can promptly correct the mistake.

STASH BUSTING!
Think of ways to use up leftover yarn, make gifts for your friends and express your creativity.

SUPERSIZE ME
When you're just starting out, super-chunky needles and yarn are great to practice with. The stitches will be big and clear and your project will grow in no time at all. Cast on 20 stitches and knit back and forth to create a garter stitch scarf.

LEARN THE ABBREVIATIONS
You'll find a list of the knitting abbreviations used in this book handily placed on the back flap for easy reference. They are also listed on page 14.

EXPERIMENT
Knitting needles come in lots of different materials: plastic, bamboo, aluminum, and wood, to name a few. Experiment with each type of needle to see which you prefer. Bamboo and wooden needles are stickier and will grip onto stitches, which is handy if you are prone to the odd dropped stitch. Aluminum and plastic needles can be slippery, but will allow you to knit faster and smoother as you gain confidence. It's all a matter of preference!

knits to wear

- Slouch hat • Ballerina slippers
- Ribbed pom–pom hat • Cozy mittens
- Seed stitch cowl • Diamond leg warmers
- Winter cape

slouch hat

This slouch hat is the ultimate quick knit. After just a few hours of knitting, you'll be winter-ready. It's a perfect starter project if you are new to knitting on circular needles.

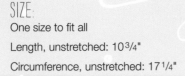

SUPPLIES

SIZE:
One size to fit all

Length, unstretched: 10 3/4"

Circumference, unstretched: 17 1/4"

YARN:
Debbie Bliss *Luxury Donegal Tweed Chunky*

Color: Heather (05)

Amount: 1 x 3 1/2 oz (100 g) ball

KNITTING NEEDLES & EXTRAS:
Size 10 1/2 (6.5 mm) circular knitting needle, 16" long

Set of four size 10 1/2 (6.5 mm) double-pointed knitting needles

Stitch marker

GAUGE:
12 sts and 19 rows to 4" measured over St st using size 10 1/2 (6.5 mm) needles.

ABBREVIATIONS:
See either page 14 or the inside back-cover flap.

TO MAKE THE SLOUCH HAT

Using circular needle, cast on 52 sts. Place a marker at beg of round and join for working in the round, being careful no stitches are twisted. (See right for tips on working in the round.)

Round 1: K52.

Continue working St st (knit every round) until work measures 10¼".

Shape crown

When knitting becomes too tight for circular needle, transfer it evenly onto three double-pointed needles and knit with the fourth needle.

Round 1: *K2tog; rep from * to end of round. (26 sts)

Round 2: *K2tog; rep from * to end of round. (13 sts)

Cut off yarn, leaving a long yarn tail. Thread the yarn tail onto a yarn needle, pass the needle through the remaining live stitches, pull to draw closed, and secure.

TO FINISH

Weave in any stray yarn ends.

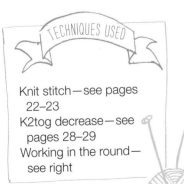

TECHNIQUES USED

Knit stitch—see pages
    22–23
K2tog decrease—see
    pages 28–29
Working in the round—
    see right

WORKING IN THE ROUND

Cast on the required number of stitches. If the stitches are twisted on the needles and wire (**1**), then untwist them and make sure they are all sitting neatly and evenly around the needle (**2**). Place a stitch marker on the right needle to indicate the beginning of the first round and knit the first stitch on the left needle to join the stitches into a round (**3**). Continue working the stitches in rounds, with the right side always facing you, and remembering to slip the stitch marker from the left needle onto the right needle at the beginning of each round (**4**).

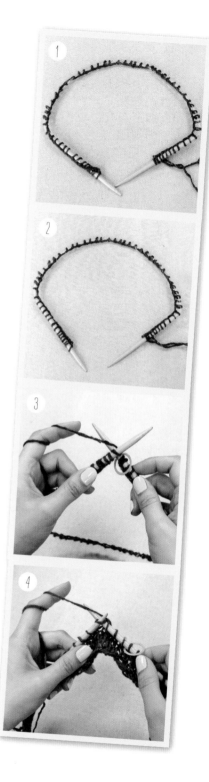

ballerina slippers

These cute, girly slippers make the perfect indoor shoes, and are deceptively simple to knit. Worked entirely on straight needles with just one seam, you can have toasty toes in no time at all.

TECHNIQUES USED

M1 increase—see pages 34–35

Ssk decrease—see page 14

K2tog decrease—see pages 28–29

Garter stitch seam—see page 49

Mattress stitch seam—see page 49

Whip stitch—see page 96

SIZE:
To fit average women's shoe sizes

Length, unstretched: 9½"

Width, unstretched: 4"

YARN:

Debbie Bliss *Rialto Chunky*

Main color: Ruby (015)

Amount: 2 x 1¾ oz (50 g) balls

KNITTING NEEDLES & EXTRAS:
Pair of size 10 (6 mm) knitting needles

Pair of size 6 (4 mm) knitting needles, for bows (optional)

Small amount of contrasting double-knitting-weight yarn, for i-cord bows (optional)

Two stitch markers and stitch holder

Two ⅝" wooden buttons

GAUGE:
13½ sts to 4" measured over garter stitch using size 10 (6 mm) needles.

ABBREVIATIONS:
See either page 14 or the inside back-cover flap.

TO MAKE THE LEFT SLIPPER
Using size 10 (6 mm) needles and main color, cast on 61 sts.
Sole
Row 1 (RS): K61.
Row 2: K1, M1, k59, M1, k1. (63 sts)
Row 3: Knit.
Row 4: K1, M1, k61, M1, k1. (65 sts)
Work 8 rows in garter st (knit every row).
Upper
Row 1 (RS): K26, place marker (pm), k13, pm, k26.
Rows 2, 4, and 6: Purl, slipping markers when reached.
Row 3: K24, ssk, slip marker (sm), k2tog, k9, ssk, sm, k2tog, k24. (61 sts)
Row 5: K23, ssk, sm, k2tog, k5, ssk, sm, k2tog, k23. (57 sts)
Row 7: K22, ssk, sm, k2tog, k1, ssk, sm, k2tog, k22. (53 sts)
Row 8: Knit.

Row 9 (RS): K10, bind off next 33 sts, k to end (10 sts now on needle after bind-off).**

Strap

Row 1 (WS): K10, cast on 15 sts onto right needle, slip remaining 10 sts onto a stitch holder. (25 sts) Turn and cont on these 25 sts only.

Row 2: K25.

Row 3 (buttonhole): K23, yo, ssk.

Row 4: K25.

Bind off all 25 sts.

Return to sts on stitch holder and with WS facing, rejoin main color and knit all 10 sts from stitch holder. Work 3 rows in garter stitch (knit every row).

Bind off.

TO MAKE THE RIGHT SLIPPER

Work as for Left Slipper to **.

Next row (WS): K10, slip remaining 10 sts onto a stitch holder. Turn and cont on these 10 sts only. Work 3 rows in garter stitch (knit every row).

Bind off.

Strap

Row 1 (WS): Using size 10 (6 mm) needles and main color, cast on 15 sts onto right needle, then with same needle and WS facing, knit all 10 sts from stitch holder. (25 sts)

Row 2: K25.

Row 3 (buttonhole): K2tog, yo, k23.

Row 4: K25.

Bind off all 25 sts.

TO SEW THE SEAMS

Fold the finished slipper piece in half lengthwise with right sides together, and sew the cast-on edges together with a simple whip stitch (see page 96). Turn the slipper right side out so the right side is facing you and use a garter stitch seam to sew the garter stitch sole of the heel. Insert the needle into the top loop of the stitch on one side and then in the bottom loop of the corresponding stitch on the other side (**1** and **2**). Continue alternating from side to side. When you reach the upper (St st) area of the slipper, switch to mattress stitch to complete the heel seam. Insert the needle under the horizontal bar between the first and second stitches and then under the bar on the corresponding stitch on the other side (**3** and **4**). Continue alternating from side to side.

TO FINISH

Sew a small button onto the outside edge of each slipper to correspond with the buttonhole.

If desired, use size 6 (4 mm) needles and contrasting double-knitting-weight yarn to make two 3-stitch i-cords 11" long for bows (see page 92). Tie in bows and sew one to the front of each slipper.

Weave in any stray yarn ends.

ribbed pom-pom hat

With wide ribbing and a folded brim, this hat is fantastically warm and snug. The classic pom–pom style means it's a great hat for both men and women to wear.

SUPPLIES

SIZE:

One size to fit women's small–medium

Length, unstretched: 10¼"

Width, unstretched: 6"

YARN:

Rowan *Wool Cotton DK*

Color choices: Celedon (979) or Misty (903)

Amount: 2 x 1¾ oz (50 g) balls for one hat

KNITTING NEEDLES & EXTRAS:

Size 5 (3.75 mm) circular knitting needle, 16" long

Set of four size 5 (3.75 mm) double-pointed knitting needles

Stitch marker

GAUGE:

22 sts and 30 rows to 4" measured over St st using size 5 (3.75 mm) needles.

ABBREVIATIONS:

See either page 14 or the inside back-cover flap.

TO MAKE THE HAT

Using circular needle and chosen color, cast on 108 sts.

Place a marker at beg of round and join for working in the round, being careful no stitches are twisted.

Round 1: *K2, p2; rep from * to end.

Repeat last round until your work measures 8¼" from cast-on edge.

Shape crown

When knitting becomes too tight for circular needle, transfer it evenly onto three double-pointed needles and knit with the fourth needle.

Round 1: *K2, p2tog, [k2, p2] twice; rep from * to end. (99 sts)

Round 2: *K2, p1, [k2, p2] twice; rep from * to end.

Round 3: Rep round 2.
Round 4: *K1, ssk, [k2, p2] twice; rep from * to end. (90 sts)
Round 5: *K4, p2, k2, p2; rep from * to end.
Round 6: Rep round 5.
Round 7: *K1, k2tog, k1, p2, k2, p2; rep from * to end. (81 sts)
Round 8: *K3, p2, k2, p2; rep from * to end.
Round 9: Rep round 8.
Round 10: *K1, k2tog, p2, k2, p2; rep from * to end. (72 sts)
Round 11: *K2, p2; rep from * to end.
Round 12: Rep round 11.
Round 13: *K2tog, p2, k2, p2; rep from * to end. (63 sts)
Round 14: *K1, p2, k2, p2; rep from * to end.
Round 15: Rep round 14.
Round 16: *K1, p2tog, k2, p2tog; rep from * to end. (45 sts)

Round 17: *K1, p1, k2tog, p1; rep from * to end. (36 sts)
Cut off yarn, leaving a long yarn tail. Thread the yarn tail onto a yarn needle, pass the needle through the remaining live stitches, pull to draw closed and secure. Leave the yarn tail to use to sew the pom–pom to the top of the hat.

TO FINISH
Make a giant pom–pom 2¾" in diameter. Using the long yarn tail on the hat, sew the pom–pom to the center of the top of the hat.
Weave in any stray yarn ends.

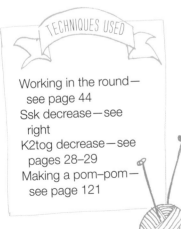

TECHNIQUES USED

Working in the round—
  see page 44
Ssk decrease—see
  right
K2tog decrease—see
  pages 28–29
Making a pom–pom—
  see page 121

WORKING THE SSK DECREASES
The ssk decreases in this pattern are worked slightly differently than the usual ssk decrease (see page 14). To work the decreases called ssk in this pattern, first slip 2 sts purlwise onto the right needle (**1** and **2**). Then insert the left needle into the fronts of the 2 slipped sts (**3**) and knit them together (**4**).

cozy mittens

You can't go wrong with a classic pair of mittens. Leave them plain or embroider them with a colorful stripe pattern or a cheeky critter. If you're prone to losing your mittens, braid or crochet a long cord, or knit a long i-cord to thread through your jacket sleeves.

SUPPLIES

SIZE:
Length, unstretched: 9"

Circumference: 7"

YARN:
Erika Knight *Vintage Wool*

Main colors: Bambi (034) for light brown pair; or Gorgeous (033) for pink pair

Amount: 1 x 1¾ oz (50 g) ball of main color makes one pair of mittens

Decoration colors: For light brown pair, scraps of DK-weight yarn in light brown, medium brown, and green, and scraps of Aran-weight yarn in medium brown, white, and black; for pink pair, scraps of Aran-weight yarn in white, pale pink, gold, and charcoal

KNITTING NEEDLES & EXTRAS:
Set of four size 8 (5 mm) double-pointed knitting needles

Set of four size 2 (2.5 mm) double-pointed knitting needles

Pair of size 6 (4 mm) knitting needles

GAUGE:
18 sts and 24 rows to 4" measured over St st using size 8 (5 mm) needles.

ABBREVIATIONS:
See either page 14 or the inside back-cover flap.

TO MAKE THE MITTENS (BOTH ALIKE)
Using size 8 (5 mm) double-pointed needles and main color, cast on 30 sts. Distribute 10 sts on each of three needles. Place a marker at beg of round and join for working in the round, being careful no stitches are twisted.

Rib round 1: *K1, p1; rep from * to end. Repeat last round until cuff measures 2¾" from cast-on edge.

Begin thumb shaping

Round 1: M1, k14, slip marker (sm), M1L, k1, M1R, sm, k15. (33 sts)

Round 2 and all even rounds: Knit.

Round 3: K15, sm, M1L, k3, M1R, sm, k15. (35 sts)

Round 5: K15, sm, M1L, k5, M1R, sm, k15. (37 sts)

Round 7: K15, sm, M1L, k7, M1R, sm, k15. (39 sts)

Round 9: K15, sm, M1L, k9, M1R, sm, k15. (41 sts)

Round 11: K15, sm, M1L, k11, M1R, sm, k15. (43 sts)

Round 13: K15, sm, M1L, k13, M1R, sm, k15. (45 sts)

Begin hand

Round 1: K15, slip next 15 sts onto a stitch holder removing markers, knit 15 rem sts by rejoining work in the round. (15 thumb sts remain unworked while hand is knitted.)

Round 2: K30.

Cont knitting every round until mitten just covers your little finger when tried on.

Shape top of hand

Rearrange sts onto just two needles (15 sts on each), removing last stitch marker.

Round 1: *K1, ssk, knit to within 3 sts of the end of needle, k2tog, k1; rep from * to end of round.

Round 2: Knit.

Rounds 3–6: [Rep rounds 1 and 2] twice. (18 sts)

Round 7: Rep round 1. (14 sts)

Graft together the 6 sts on each needle, using Kitchener stitch to finish the hand (see page 85).

Complete thumb

Using size 8 (5 mm) double-pointed needles, distribute 15 thumb stitches evenly on three needles (5 sts on each needle) and with RS facing, join for working in round. Using main color, knit every round until work covers all but the very tip

of your thumb when tried on.

Shape top of thumb

Round 1: *K3, k2tog; rep from * to end of round. (12 sts)

Round 2: Knit.

Round 3: *K2, k2tog; rep from * to end of round. (9 sts)

Round 4: Knit.

Round 5: *K1, k2tog; rep from * to end of round. (6 sts)

Cut off yarn, leaving a long yarn tail. Thread the yarn tail onto a yarn needle, pass the needle through the remaining live stitches, pull to draw closed, and secure.

Weave in any stray yarn ends.

TO BLOCK THE MITTENS

Wet block the pair of mittens as explained on page 104, patting the wet mittens into shape on a towel and leaving them to dry.

Once the work is completely dry, work the embellishment of your choice, making the acorns and leaves for the light brown pair only.

TO MAKE THE ACORNS

Using a medium brown DK-weight yarn and a set of size 2 (2.5 mm) double-pointed needles, cast on 4 sts. Distribute sts over three needles.

Round 1: [Kfb] 4 times. (8 sts)

Round 2: Knit.

Round 3: [Kfb, k1] 4 times. (12 sts)

Rounds 4, 5, 6, 7, and 8: Knit.

Round 9: Change to light brown

DK-weight yarn, kfb in each st. (24 sts)

Redistribute sts evenly on three needles (8 sts on each needle).

Round 10: Purl.

Round 11: K1, p1; rep from * to end.

Round 12: Work in seed st and decrease as follows—[p1, k1] 3 times, p2tog; rep from * twice more. (21 sts)

Round 13: Work in seed st and decrease as follows—[k1, p1] twice, k1, p2tog; rep from * twice more. (18 sts)

Round 14: [P2tog] 9 times. (9 sts) Stuff acorn with scraps of yarn.

Round 15: [P2tog] 4 times, p1. (5 sts)

Round 16: P1, p2tog twice. (3 sts)**

Knit a 12" i-cord on these 3 sts (see page 92) and bind off.

Make a second acorn and i-cord in exactly the same way.

Then make two acorns as for first acorn to ** and finish as follows:

Round 17: P2tog and fasten off. Thread an i-cord through the top of the ribbing on each mitten as shown. Sew a second acorn to the other end of each i-cord.

TO MAKE THE ACORN LEAVES

Using size 6 (4 mm) needles and green DK-weight yarn, cast on 3 sts.

Row 1: Knit.

Row 2 and all even rows: Knit.

Row 3: Kfb, p1, kfb. (5 sts)

Row 5: Kfb, k1, p1, k1, kfb. (7 sts)

Row 7: Kfb, k2, p1, k2, kfb. (9 sts)

Row 9: K2tog, k2, p1, k2, k2tog. (7 sts)

Row 11: K2tog, k1, p1, k1, k2tog. (5 sts)

Row 13: Rep row 5. (7 sts)

Row 15: Rep row 7. (9 sts)

Row 17: Kfb, k3, p1, k3, kfb. (11 sts)

Row 19: K2tog, k3, p1, k3, k2tog. (9 sts)

Row 21: Rep row 9. (7 sts)

Row 23: Rep row 7. (9 sts)

Row 25: Rep row 17. (11 sts)

Row 27: Kfb, k4, p1, k4, kfb. (13 sts)

Row 29: Kfb, k5, p1, k5, kfb. (15 sts)

Row 31: K2tog, k5, p1, k5, k2tog. (13 sts)

Row 33: K2tog, k4, p1, k4, k2tog. (11 sts)

Row 34: K2tog, knit to last 2 sts, k2tog. (9 sts)

Row 35: K2tog, k2, p1, k2, k2tog. (7 sts)

Row 37: Kfb, k2, p1, k2, kfb. (9 sts)

Row 39: K3, turn work, k3, turn work, k2tog, k1, turn work, k2tog and fasten off.
Rejoin yarn to RS, k1, p1, k1, turn work, k3, turn work, k1, p1, k1, turn work, k2tog, k1, turn work, k2tog and fasten off.
Rejoin yarn to RS, k3, turn work, k3, turn work, k2tog, k1, turn work, k2tog and fasten off.
Make three more leaves in the same way and sew two to each acorn.

TO EMBROIDER THE MITTENS

To work the squirrel in duplicate stitch on the light brown pair, follow the chart below, centering the squirrel on the front of each mitten and reversing one to face in the opposite direction. For the embroidery on the pink pair, work three stripes in duplicate stitch across the front 15 stitches of the mittens only, working the first row 4 rows above the ribbing and the other two 5 rows apart. Use white, pink, gold, and charcoal yarns alternately for the stitches across the stripe. Work five French knots between the stripes as shown.

TECHNIQUES USED

Working in the round—see page 44

Ssk decrease—see page 14

K2tog decrease—see pages 28–29

Kfb increase—see pages 32–33

Duplicate stitch—see page 104

IMPORTANT NOTE

The duplicate-stitch squirrel is actually worked upside down on the mittens, so turn the chart upside down when embroidering the motif.

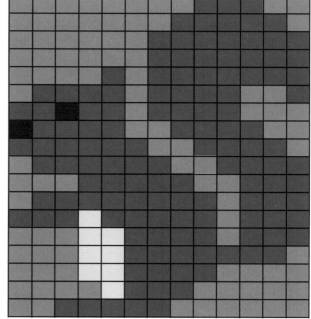

KEY

☐ White

☐ Medium brown

■ Black

☐ Bambi

58

OTHER IDEAS

WHETHER YOU LOVE CUTE WOODLAND CRITTERS OR COLORFUL POLKA DOTS, CUSTOMIZE YOUR MITTENS TO MAKE THEM UNIQUE.

seed stitch cowl

There is nothing better than a big, squishy cowl to keep you warm. This pattern uses a gorgeous super-bulky yarn and a dense seed stitch. Just keep going until you run out of yarn—the bigger the better, I say.

SIZE:
Circumference: 43¾"
Width: 9"

YARN:
Erika Knight *Maxi Wool*
Color: Artisan (020)
Amount: 2 x 3½ oz (100 g) balls

KNITTING NEEDLES & EXTRAS:
Size 15 (10 mm) circular knitting needle, 16" long

Stitch marker

TECHNIQUES USED

Working in the round—
see page 44
Seed stitch—see right

GAUGE:
9 sts and 17½ rows to 4" measured over seed stitch pattern using size 15 (10 mm) needles.

ABBREVIATIONS:
See either page 14 or the inside back-cover flap.

TO MAKE THE COWL
Cast on 100 sts.
Place a marker at beg of round and join for working in the round, being careful no stitches are twisted.
Round 1: *K1, p1; rep from * to end.
Round 2: *P1, k1; rep from * to end.
Last two rounds are repeated to form seed st pattern.
Cont in seed st until your work measures approximately 9" from cast-on edge, or until you run out of yarn.
Bind off knitwise.

TO FINISH
Weave in any stray yarn ends.
Do not press.

WORKING SEED STITCH
While working seed stitch, when you change from a knit to a purl stitch, you must be sure that the yarn is in the correct position to work the next stitch. When knitting a stitch the yarn is always held at the back of the work and when purling a stitch the yarn is always held at the front of the work.

diamond leg warmers

Knitted in a scrumptious, textured diamond pattern using only knit and purl stitches, these leg warmers are fantastic when you need that extra bit of comfort inside a pair of rubber boots or some snuggly warmth on a winter's day.

SUPPLIES

SIZE:
Circumference, unstretched: 9$\frac{1}{2}$"

Width, unstretched: 4$\frac{3}{4}$"

Length: 11$\frac{3}{4}$"

YARN
Rico *Essentials Soft Merino Aran*

Color: Mandarin (070)

Amount: 2 x 1$\frac{3}{4}$ oz (50 g) balls

KNITTING NEEDLES & EXTRAS:
Set of four size 8 (5 mm) double-pointed knitting needles

Stitch marker

GAUGE:
17 sts and 24 rows to 4" measured over diamond stitch pattern using size 8 (5 mm) needles.

ABBREVIATIONS:
See either page 14 or the inside back-cover flap.

TO MAKE THE LEG WARMERS

Cast on 40 sts.

Distribute sts onto three double-pointed needles (13 on needle one, 13 on needle two, 14 on needle three).

Place a marker at beg of round and join for working in the round, being careful no stitches are twisted.

Rib round 1: *K1, p1; rep from * to end.

Repeat last round 5 times more. (A total of 6 rib rounds have been worked.)

Next round: *K1, p1; rep from * to end, M1. (41 sts)

Begin diamond pattern

Round 1: K4, [p1, k7] 4 times (5 sts remain), p1, k4.

Round 2: K3, [p1, k1, p1, k5] 4 times (6 sts remain), p1, k1, p1, k3.

Round 3: K2, [p1, k3] 9 times (3 sts remain), p1, k2.

Round 4: K1, *p1, k5, p1, k1; rep from * to end.

Round 5: [P1, k7] 5 times (1 st remains), p1.

Round 6: Rep round 4.

Round 7: Rep round 3.

Round 8: Rep round 2.

Rounds 1–8 are repeated to form the pattern.

[Repeat rounds 1–8] 6 times more. (A total of seven 8-round pattern repeats have been worked.)

Repeat pattern round 1 once more to complete the pattern.

Next round: K2tog, p1, *k1, p1; rep from * to end.

Next round: *K1, p1; rep from * to end.

Repeat last round 5 times more. Bind off in rib.

Make a second leg warmer in the same way.

TO FINISH

Weave in any stray yarn ends.

TO SPRAY BLOCK THE LEG WARMERS

To really bring this stitch pattern to life, it is essential that you spray block the knitting.

Lay a clean, dry bath towel on a flat surface. Place each leg warmer on this towel and pin evenly to a width of 4¾" and a length of 11¾". Using a spray bottle filled with water, spritz the knitting until wet through.

Leave the leg warmers to dry overnight.

TECHNIQUES *USED*

Knit stitch—see pages 22–23

Purl stitch—see pages 24–25

M1 increase—see pages 34–35

K2tog decrease— see pages 28–29

Spray blocking— see right

winter cape

Reminiscent of a traditional raglan sweater, this super-soft cape is knitted from the top down on circular needles and shaped with basic increases. A great starting point if you want to slowly graduate to the world of sweater knitting.

SIZE:
Length from top of shoulder to bottom edge of cape: 18^1/$_2$"

Circumference around bottom edge of cape: 44^1/$_2$"

Turtleneck, unstretched: length 8", width 8", circumference 16"

YARN
Rico *Creative Twist Super Chunky*

Color: Charcoal (05)

Amount: 4 x 3^1/$_2$ oz (100 g) balls

KNITTING NEEDLES & EXTRAS:
Size 15 (10 mm) circular knitting needle, 16" long

Size 15 (10 mm) circular knitting needle, 32" long

Size 15 (10 mm) circular knitting needle, 40" long

Four stitch markers

GAUGE:
8^1/$_2$ sts and 12 rows to 4" measured over St st using size 15 (10 mm) needles.

ABBREVIATIONS:
See either page 14 or the inside back-cover flap.

TECHNIQUES USED
Working in the round—see page 44
K1, p1 ribbing—see page 68
Kfb increase—see pages 32–33
Spray blocking—see page 65

67

TO MAKE THE CAPE

Using 16"-long circular needle, cast on 40 sts.

Place a marker at beg of round and join for working in the round, being careful no stitches are twisted.

Turtleneck

The cape is begun at the top of the turtleneck.

Rib round 1: *K1, p1; rep from * to end.

Repeat last round 21 times more, placing a marker after every 10 sts on last rib round. (It is a good idea to use different color markers than the one used at the beginning of the round, so you can keep track of your rounds easily.)

Shape shoulders

As you continue to increase stitches at the shoulders, your work will grow and, at various stages, you will need to transfer your stitches onto the longer circular needles. By the time you finish increasing you should be using the 40" circular needle.

Begin increasing as follows:

Round 1: Kfb, [k to within 1 st of marker, kfb, slip marker, kfb] 3 times, k to last st at end of round, kfb. (8 sts increased in round)

Round 2: Knit.

Repeat last two rounds 6 times more. (96 sts)

Work in St st (knit every round) without shaping for 38 rounds more (approximately 12½" more).

Next round: *K1, p1; rep from * to end.

Repeat last round 4 times more. Bind off knitwise.

TO FINISH

Weave in any stray yarn ends. Spray block cape on a flat surface, paying particular attention to the increase seams at the shoulder and leave to dry overnight. This will encourage a lovely, silky drape when the cape is worn.

WORKING KNIT ONE, PURL ONE RIB

When knitting a stitch, the yarn is always held at the back of the work and when purling a stitch, the yarn is always held at the front of the work. While working a k1, p1 ribbing, you must change the position of the yarn after each stitch. After working a knit stitch, take the yarn to the front of the work between the two needles so you are ready to purl the next stitch (**1**). After working a purl stitch, take the yarn to the back of the work between the two needles so you are ready to knit the next stitch (**2**). The finished k1, p1 rib forms vertical ridges (**3**).

When moving the yarn from the back to the front, or from the front to the back, make sure the yarn is passed between the two needles rather than over them.

knits to share

- Maiden braid bracelet • Bow necklace
- Cell phone case • Cable headband
- Coin purse • Pom–pom necklace
- Bowwow bow tie

maiden braid bracelet

Simply a stand-alone cable braid, these bangles remind me of oversized friendship bracelets. If you are new to knitting cables, these bracelets are fantastic practice pieces.

SUPPLIES

SIZE:

Circumference around outside of bracelet: 8³/₄"

Width: 1"

Note: Bracelet circumference is adjustable.

YARN:

King Cole *Bamboo Cotton DK*

Main color choices: Pebble (610) or Yellow (523)

Amount: Approximately ³/₄ oz (20 g) for each bracelet

KNITTING NEEDLES & EXTRAS:

Pair of size 5 (3.75 mm) knitting needles

Extra knitting needle for three-needle bind-off—size 5 (3.75 mm) or smaller

Size F/5 (4 mm) crochet hook

Cable needle

Small amount of scrap yarn in a contrasting color for provisional cast-on

GAUGE:

It is not necessary to work this bracelet to an exact gauge.

ABBREVIATIONS:

C12F slip next 6 sts onto cable needle and hold at front of work, knit next 6 sts, then knit 6 sts from cable needle.

C12B slip next 6 sts onto cable needle and hold at back of work, knit next 6 sts, then knit 6 sts from cable needle.

See also either page 14 or the inside back-cover flap.

TECHNIQUES USED

Provisional crochet-chain cast-on or open cast-on— see page 74
Front and back cables
Three-needle bind-off

TO MAKE THE BRACELET

Using a crochet hook and contrasting scrap yarn, make 18 chain stitches and fasten off, then tie a knot in the yarn tail at this end—this will come in handy later! Using knitting needles and main color yarn, pick up and knit one st in each of the chain sts. (18 sts) Alternatively, cast on 18 sts using the open cast-on method (see right). Begin cable pattern as follows:

Row 1: K18.
Row 2: P18.
Row 3: C12F, k6.
Row 4: P18.
Row 5: K18.
Row 6: P18.
Row 7: K6, C12B.
Row 8: P18.
Row 9: K18.
Row 10: P18.
[Repeat rows 3–10] 6 times more, then work rows 3–8 only for the last (eighth) repeat.
Set aside—do not bind off and do not cut off yarn.

TO ADJUST THE LENGTH

For a longer (or shorter) bracelet, alter the number of cable repeats. Make sure you work only cable rows 3–8 for the last repeat. This ensures the braid is continuously joined.

TO FINISH

Join the ends of the bracelet together with three-needle bind-off (see right). Weave in any stray yarn ends and turn the bracelet right side out.

WORKING THE THREE-NEEDLE BIND-OFF

With the right side of the work facing you and the cast-on edge at the top, work from right to left and slip each picked-up stitch from the crochet chain onto an extra knitting needle. Find that knotted end of the chain and undo the very last stitch—you should be able to pull gently on the tail and watch the chain unzip neatly. (I find this very satisfying!) You will see you have the same number of live stitches at either end of the knitting. Bring the two needles together so that the right sides of the knitting are together and the wrong sides are facing outward. Hold the two needles in the left hand ready to start the bind-off. This bind-off method leaves a ridge, but it will be hidden on the inside. Using a third needle, bind off all stitches in the usual way but inserting the right needle through one stitch on each left needle as you bind off.

WORKING THE OPEN CAST-ON

Cut a strand of contrasting yarn. With the working yarn, make a slip knot and place it on two needles (**1**). Holding the waste yarn under the slip knot, take the working yarn under the waste yarn and over the needles from front to back, then bring the working yarn in front of the waste yarn (**2**). Repeat step 2 until all the stitches are cast on (**3**). Take out one needle before knitting the first row (**4**). Remove the waste yarn only when you are ready to pick up stitches along this cast-on edge.

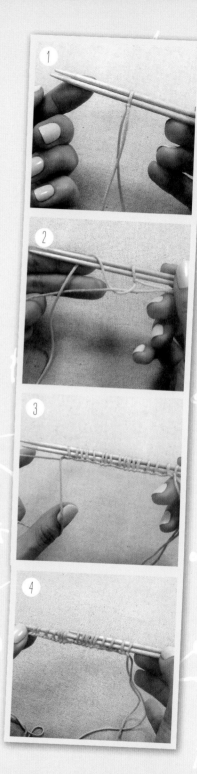

bow necklace

These bow necklaces were one of the first knits I ever designed. They are delicate and oh-so cute. As well as adding them to a necklace chain, try attaching them to other jewelry findings, such as a brooch pin or a ring, to create a whole set.

SIZE:
Across finished bow: 1¹/₂"

Bow width: 1"

YARN:
Sirdar *Snuggly Baby Bamboo DK*

Color choices: Light Blue (169), Shrimpy (119), or Perky Pink (124)

King Cole *Bamboo Cotton DK*

Color choice: Mint (517)

Amount: Approximately ¹/₄ oz (5 g) for one bow

KNITTING NEEDLES & EXTRAS:
Pair of size 5 (3.75 mm) knitting needles

18" necklace chain with clasp

Two 4 mm jump rings

Two pairs of slim jewelry pliers

GAUGE:
It is not necessary to work the bow to an exact gauge.

ABBREVIATIONS:
See either page 14 or the inside back-cover flap.

TO MAKE THE BOW
Using chosen color, cast on 18 sts.

Work 10 rows in garter stitch (knit every row).

Bind off, leaving a long yarn tail. Thread the yarn tail onto a yarn needle. Bring the two side edges together and sew the seam using the garter stitch seam method (see page 49).

Weave in any stray yarn ends.

Fold the bow with the seam at the center back.

Pinch the center of the bow together and firmly wrap a long length of yarn several times around the middle.

Tie a double knot to secure and weave in the yarn ends.

TO ASSEMBLE THE NECKLACE
Using two pairs of slim jewelry pliers, open the jump rings and loop them onto a stitch halfway up the inside of each side of the bow, without closing shut. Lay the necklace chain through the jump ring on one side, and close it. Pass one end of the chain through the center wrap of the bow and pull it through gently until the lengths of chain are even. Lay the chain through the remaining open jump ring and close it to secure.

cell Phone case

This case really has it all, aside from protecting your phone from bumps and scratches, it has a protective strap to hold the phone in place and a nifty pocket to stash your cards and cash. What more could you need?

SIZE:
Width, unstretched: 2¹/₂"

Length: 5" (adjustable)

YARN:
Rico *Essentials Merino DK*

Color choices: Natural (60) and Wood (53) for white and brown case; or Natural (60) and Yellow (65) for white and yellow case

Amounts: 1 x 1³/₄ oz (50 g) ball in wood or yellow and a small amount in natural

KNITTING NEEDLES & EXTRAS:
Set of four size 5 (3.75 mm) double-pointed knitting needles

Stitch marker

Size E/4 (3.5 mm) crochet hook

One ⁵/₈" button

GAUGE:
24 sts and 34 rows to 4" measured over St st using size 5 (3.75 mm) needles.

ABBREVIATIONS:
See either page 14 or the inside back-cover flap.

TO MAKE THE CASE
Using double-pointed needles and natural, cast on 32 sts. Distribute sts evenly on three needles (8 sts on each needle). Place a marker at beg of round and join for working in the round, being careful no stitches are twisted.

Rib round 1: *K1, p1; rep from * to end.

Repeat last round until ribbing measures ³/₄" from cast-on edge.

TECHNIQUES USED

Three-needle bind-off—see page 74
Picking up stitches on St st—see page 81
Mattress stitch—see page 49
Crochet chain

Change to wood or yellow and work in St st (knit every round) for a further 4¼", or until knitting covers your device.

Cut off yarn, leaving a very long length of yarn for binding off.

Turn knitting wrong side out. With the working yarn at the tip of one of the needles, redistribute the sts onto two knitting needles (16 sts on each needle).

Bring the two needles together so that the right sides of the knitting are together and the wrong sides are facing outward. Hold the two needles in the left hand ready to start the bind-off.

Using a third needle, bind off all stitches in the usual way but inserting the right needle through one stitch on each left needle as you bind off.

Turn the case right side out.

TO MAKE THE POCKET

Decide which side of the case you want the pocket on. There are 16 sts across each side of the case and you will be picking up 14 sts across the case, so start picking up the stitches one stitch in from the right side-edge at the bottom of the case—and four rows up from the seam. When picking up the stitches hold the case with the ribbing at the top. To pick up the first stitch, insert a size 5 (3.75 mm) knitting needle from right to left under the second

leg of the two legs of the V-shaped stitch. Working horizontally across the bottom of the case, pick up one stitch in each of the next 13 stitches in the same way, so you now have 14 stitches on the needle (**1** and **2**). With WS facing, beg with a purl row (**3**) and work in St st (working one purl row and one knit row alternately) until the pocket measures 2¾", ending with a purl (WS) row.

Next row: [K1, p1] to end.
Repeat last row 3 times more.
Bind off.

Align the edge of the pocket flap with the adjacent column of stitches on the case and use mattress stitch to invisibly join the two pieces. Repeat this on both sides of the pocket.

Weave in any stray yarn ends.

TO MAKE THE STRAP

Sew the button to the pocket just below the ribbing.

Using a crochet hook and natural, insert the hook around the center stitch at the bottom of the ribbing on the back of the case, wrap the yarn around the hook and pull a loop through. Work 40 chain stitches or until the chain reaches the top of the case, down around the button and back to the beginning of the chain. Fasten off and sew to the end of the first chain.

Weave in any stray yarn ends.

cable headband

Perfect for keeping your ears warm without ruining your hairdo, this delightful twisted cable headband is knitted flat and then grafted together with an invisible seam.

SIZE:
Circumference, unstretched: $18^1/_2$"

Width: 4"

Note: Headband circumference is adjustable.

YARN:
Rico *Essentials Big*

Color: Coral (017)

Amount: 1 x $1^3/_4$ oz (50 g) ball

KNITTING NEEDLES & EXTRAS:
Pair of size 11 (8 mm) knitting needles

L/11 (8 mm) crochet hook

Cable needle

Small amount of scrap yarn in a contrasting color for provisional cast-on

GAUGE:
It is not necessary to work this headband to an exact gauge.

ABBREVIATIONS:

C12F slip next 6 sts onto cable needle and hold at front of work, knit next 6 sts, then knit 6 sts from cable needle.

C12B slip next 6 sts onto cable needle and hold at back of work, knit next 6 sts, then knit 6 sts from cable needle.

See also either page 14 or the inside back-cover flap.

TO MAKE THE HEADBAND
Using crochet hook and contrasting scrap yarn, make 18 chain stitches and fasten off. Using knitting needles and main color, pick up and knit one st in each of the chain sts. (18 sts)

Row 1: K18.

Row 2: P18.

Continue working in St st until work measures $6^1/_4$" from cast-on edge.

Cable pattern
Begin 8-row cable pattern as follows:

Row 1: C12F, k6.

Rows 2, 4, 6, and 8: P18.

Rows 3 and 7: K18.

Row 5: K6, C12B.

Repeat cable pattern rows 1–8 twice more.

Beg with a knit row, work in St st (knit one row, purl one row alternately) for $6^1/_4$".

If necessary, adjust length of headband before cutting off yarn.

Do not bind off.

Cut off yarn, leaving a long yarn tail to work the Kitchener stitch seam.

TO FINISH
With the right side of the knitting facing you and the cast-on edge at the top, work from right to left and slip each picked up stitches from the crochet chain onto an extra knitting needle and remove the waste yarn. You will see you have the same number of live stitches at either end of the knitting. Graft together the two ends of the headband with a Kitchener stitch seam (see page 85).

WORKING A KITCHENER STITCH SEAM

Thread a blunt-tipped yarn needle with the long yarn tail. Hold the two knitting needles together parallel, with wrong sides facing, and the needle from which the long tail comes at the back. * Insert the needle purlwise into the first stitch on the front knitting needle (**1**). Pull the yarn through, leaving the stitch on the knitting needle. Insert the needle knitwise into the first stitch on the back knitting needle (**2**). Pull the yarn through, leaving the stitch on the knitting needle. Insert the needle knitwise into the first stitch on the front needle (**3**). Slip the stitch off the needle. Insert the needle purlwise into the next stitch on the front needle (**4**). Pull the yarn through, leaving the stitch on the needle. Insert the needle purlwise into the first stitch on the back needle (**5**). Slip the stitch off the needle. Insert the needle knitwise into the next stitch on the back needle. Pull the yarn through, leaving the stitch on the needle. Repeat from * until all the stitches have been grafted (**6** and **7**). Weave in any stray yarn ends.

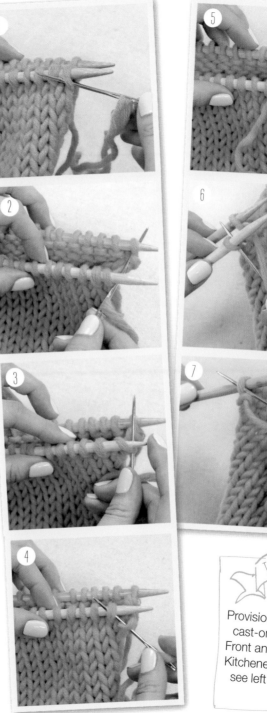

TECHNIQUES USED

Provisional crochet-chain cast-on
Front and back cables
Kitchener stitch seam—see left

coin purse

When I was eight years old my grandma gave me a coin purse just like this one, which I carried everywhere. It's the prettiest pouch for your loose change and the knitted lining makes it extra strong and durable.

SUPPLIES

SIZE:

Width across top: 3"

Length from top edge to base: 2³/₄"

YARN:

Erika Knight *Blue Wool*

Colors: Iced Gem (041) and Milk (036)

Amounts: 1 x ⁷/₈ oz (25 g) ball of each color

KNITTING NEEDLES & EXTRAS:

Set of five size 6 (4 mm) double-pointed knitting needles

Stitch marker and stitch holder

3" metal coin purse frame

Fabric glue and toothpicks

GAUGE:

22 sts and 30 rows to 4" measured over St st using size 6 (4 mm) needles.

ABBREVIATIONS:

See either page 14 or the inside back-cover flap.

TO MAKE THE PURSE

Using iced gem and double-pointed needles, cast on 15 sts onto one needle.

Purse base

Using two needles and beg with a knit row, work 7 rows in St st (knit one row, purl one row alternately), so ending with a knit row.

Purse sides

Leave the sts on your needle and use three new needles to pick up and knit 7 sts along one side edge, 15 sts along the cast-on edge, and 7 sts along the other side. (44 sts)

Place a marker at beg of round and join for working in the round, taking care no stitches are twisted.

Work in St st (knit every round) until your purse measures 1¹/₂" from pick-up round.

Next round: K17, k2tog, k20, k2tog, leaving the last 3 sts unworked. (42 sts)

Shape top of purse

Rearrange your sts onto just two needles—slip the last 3 unworked sts and next 18 sts onto one needle and slip remaining 21 sts onto a stitch holder.

**Work back and forth in rows on the 21 sts on the needle as follows:

Row 1 (RS): Ssk, knit to last 2 sts, k2tog. (19 sts)

Purl 1 row, knit 1 row, purl 1 row.

Row 5: Ssk, knit to last 2 sts, k2tog. (17 sts)

Purl 1 row.

Row 7: Ssk, knit to last 2 sts, k2tog. (15 sts)

Do not bind off. Cut off yarn, leaving sts on a spare needle.**

Return to sts on holder, and with RS facing, rejoin yarn and work as first side from ** to **.

TO MAKE THE LINING

Using milk and double-pointed needles, cast on 13 sts.

Lining base

Using two needles and beg with a knit row, work 5 rows in St st, so ending with a knit row.

Lining sides

Leave the sts on your needle and use three new needles to pick up and knit 6 sts along one side edge, 13 sts along the cast-on edge, and 6 sts along the other side. (38 sts)

Place a marker at beg of round and join in the round.

Work in St st (knit every round) until your lining measures 1¹/₂" from pick-up round.

Next round: K35, leaving the last 3 sts unworked.

Shape top of lining

Rearrange your sts onto just two needles—slip the last 3 unworked sts and next 16 sts onto one needle and slip remaining 19 sts onto a stitch holder.

***Work back and forth in rows on the 19 sts on the needle as follows:

Row 1 (RS): Ssk, knit to last 2 sts, k2tog. (17 sts)

Purl 1 row, knit 1 row, purl 1 row.

Row 5: Ssk, knit to last 2 sts, k2tog. (15 sts)

Purl 1 row.

Do not bind off. Cut off yarn, leaving sts on needle.***

Return to sts on holder, and with RS facing, rejoin yarn and work as first side from *** to ***.

TO JOIN THE PURSE AND THE LINING

Turn the lining inside out and arrange it inside the purse piece.

Slip the sts of each side of purse onto a double-pointed needle. Hold purse and lining sts on one side together with purse side facing you. Using a third needle and iced gem, bind off in the usual way but inserting right needle through one st on each left needle as you bind off. Use the yarn tails of your bind-off to sew the side edges together.

Use the three-needle bind-off to join the other side in the same way. Weave in any remaining yarn ends. Using a toothpick, spread the fabric glue into the space of one side of the purse frame, so the whole surface is covered. Gently maneuver one side of the purse into the frame from one end to the other, using a clean toothpick to push the edges as far as they will go. Leave the glue to dry for the required time before attaching the other side.

pom–pom necklace

Inspired by a pom–pom garland I made to brighten up my work studio, this necklace adds a big helping of whimsy to your outfit. Make the pom–poms as big as you dare!

SUPPLIES

SIZE:
Circumference of necklace: 27^1/$_2$"

Pom–pom: 1^1/$_2$" in diameter

YARN:
Debbie Bliss *Cashmerino Aran*

Colors: Charcoal (028), White (025) and Kingfisher (062)

Amount: Approximately ^{3}/$_4$ oz (20 g) of each color

KNITTING NEEDLES & EXTRAS:
Two size 5 (3.75 mm) double-pointed knitting needles

^{3}/$_4$" pom–pom maker or cardboard to make templates

GAUGE:
It is not necessary to work the i-cord chain to an exact gauge.

ABBREVIATIONS:
See either page 14 or the inside back-cover flap.

TECHNIQUES USED

Knitting an i-cord—see page 92
Making pom–poms—see page 121

TO MAKE THE NECKLACE CHAIN

Using charcoal, knit a 16" long i-cord as explained right.
Bind off, leaving a 12" yarn tail.
Weave in the short yarn tail at the cast-on end of the i-cord.

TO MAKE THE POM-POMS

Using a pom–pom maker, make two 1½" pom–poms in charcoal, three in white, and two in kingfisher. If you do not have a pom–pom maker, make the pom–poms with two cardboard rings (see page 121). To make really dense, fluffy pom–poms, wrap the yarn around lots of times before you tie and cut them. Trim carefully with sharp embroidery scissors to even up the edges.

TO ASSEMBLE THE NECKLACE

To bring your necklace to life, thread the long yarn tail on your i-cord through a yarn needle and carefully pass it through the center of a charcoal pom–pom, a white pom–pom, a kingfisher pom–pom, a white pom–pom, a kingfisher pom–pom, a white pom–pom, and a charcoal pom–pom. Now take the opposite end of your i-cord and thread the yarn tail through its center for 4"–6", pulling the pom–poms as close as possible to the end of the i-cord. Weave the yarn tail into the i-cord to secure it.

MAKING AN I-CORD

Cast on 3 sts onto one double-pointed needle (**1**).
Use a second double-pointed needle to knit the i-cord as follows:
Round 1: K3.
Round 2: Without turning your work, slide all 3 stitches to the opposite end of your needle, pass the working yarn behind the stitches and k3 (**2**).
Repeat last round until your i-cord measures the required length (**3**), then bind off.

bowwow bow tie

Not just for dogs, this dapper bow tie will add some serious suave to any neckline. There is some very basic sewing involved, but if I can do it, you can do it, too!

SUPPLIES

SIZE:
Across finished bow: 5½"

Bow width: 2¾"

Strap circumference: Adjustable

YARN:
Sirdar *Flirt DK*

Color: Mesmerize (216)

Amount: 1 x 1¾ oz (50 g)

KNITTING NEEDLES & EXTRAS:
Pair of size 6 (4 mm) knitting needles

15" length of ¾" black elastic

Bow tie "hook and eye" fastening

Sewing needle and black cotton sewing thread

GAUGE:
It is not necessary to work the bow to an exact gauge.

ABBREVIATIONS:
See either page 14 or the inside back-cover flap.

TO MAKE THE BOW
Cast on 60 sts.
Work 30 rows in garter stitch (knit every row).
Bind off, leaving a 12" yarn tail.
Thread the long yarn tail onto a blunt-tipped yarn needle. Fold the knitting in half lengthwise and sew the short side edges together.
Weave in any stray yarn ends.

TO MAKE THE BOW-TIE CENTER
Cast on 10 sts.
Beg with a k row, work 14 rows in St st (knit one row, purl one row alternately).
Bind off, leaving a 12" yarn tail.
Thread the long yarn tail onto a blunt-tipped yarn needle. Sew the cast-on edge to the bound-off edge using basic whip stitch (see page 96).
Weave in any stray yarn ends.

TO ASSEMBLE THE COLLAR

Fold the bow piece in half with the right sides together and the seam at the center back. Pass the bow through the center piece, unfolding as you proceed, and manipulate it into a traditional bow shape. Feed the length of black elastic through the back of the bow center. Slip one end of the elastic strap through the hook section of the fastenings, with the hook facing outward, and sew it back to the strap using a sewing needle and black thread. Thread the other end through the adjustor section first, facing outward, then through the eye section, pulling it long and doubling back through the back of the adjustor section. Fold the raw edge of the elastic back on itself and sew in place to secure.

TECHNIQUES USED

Garter stitch
Stockinette stitch
Whip stitch—see right

OTHER IDEAS

WHY NOT TRY ADDING THIS KNITTED BOW TO A HEADBAND TO MAKE A CUTE HAIR BOW, OR LOOP IT OVER A BELT TO ACCESSORIZE AN OUTFIT.

WORKING A WHIP STITCH SEAM

Place the knitted piece with wrong sides together (**1**). Thread a blunt-tipped yarn needle with the long tail of yarn. Insert the yarn needle through the front edge, taking it through the back edge at a diagonal angle (**2**). Continue passing the needle through both front and back edges at a diagonal until the seam is sewn (**3**). Weave in any stray yarn ends.

Knits for your home

- Flamingo pillow • Triangle motif throw
- Cotton dishcloth • Chevron pillow
- Egg cozy caps • Porcupine paperweight

flamingo pillow

Flamingos, I hear, get their pink color from the algae they eat in their natural watery habitat. This fine feathery friend is embroidered on the pillow after it has been knitted, using duplicate stitch. No algae needed!

SIZE:
Width: 16"

Length: 16"

YARN:
Debbie Bliss *Cashmerino Aran*

Colors: Gray (009), Rose (053), White (025), and Black (300)

Amounts: 3 x 1³/₄ oz (50 g) balls in gray, 1 x 1³/₄ oz (50 g) ball in rose, and a small amount each in white and black

KNITTING NEEDLES & EXTRAS:
Pair of size 8 (5 mm) knitting needles

Three 1³/₈" buttons

16" x 16" pillow form

GAUGE:
18 sts and 24 rows to 4" measured over St st using size 8 (5 mm) needles.

ABBREVIATIONS:
See either page 14 or the inside back-cover flap.

SPECIAL NOTE:
The pillow cover is worked in stockinette stitch with a ribbed border along the edges of the back opening. Once the pillow has been completed the flamingo is worked in duplicate stitch on the front.

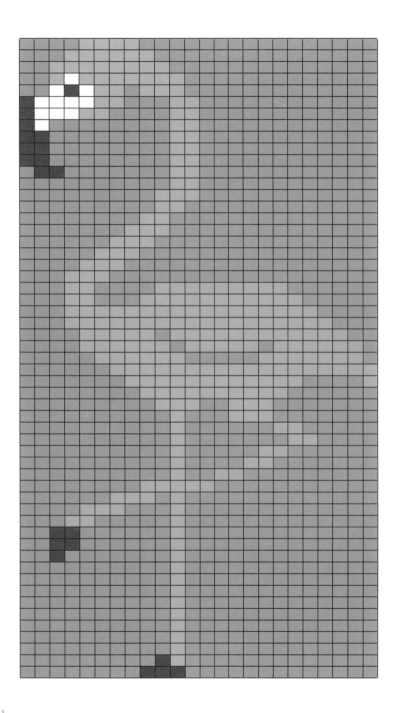

TO MAKE THE PILLOW COVER

Using gray, cast on 72 sts.
Begin k1, p1 ribbing as follows:
Rib row 1: *K1, p1; rep from * to end.
Repeat last row 8 times more. (A total of 9 rib rows have been worked.)
Beg working in St st as follows:
Row 1 (RS): Knit.
Row 2: Purl.
Repeat last 2 rows until your work measures 32" from the cast-on edge, ending with a purl (WS) row.
Next row (RS): *K1, p1; rep from * to end.
Work 3 rows more in k1, p1 ribbing as set, so ending with a WS row.
Buttonholes
Keeping the rib correct as set, work buttonholes over next 2 rows as follows (see next page for further explanation):
Buttonhole row 1 (RS): Rib 15 sts, bind off next 4 sts, *work in rib until there are 15 sts on right needle after last bind-off, bind off next 4 sts; rep from * once more, rib to end.
Buttonhole row 2: Keeping rib correct as set, *rib 15 sts, turn work, cast on 4 sts onto the left needle using the knit-on cast-on, turn work: rep from * twice more, rib to end.
Work 3 rows more in rib. Bind off.

KEY

Rose
Black
Gray
White

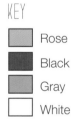

WORKING THE BUTTONHOLES

On the first buttonhole row, work in rib to the position of the buttonhole and then bind off the next 4 stitches in the usual way (**1**, **2**, and **3**).

Repeat these steps for each subequent buttonhole and then work in rib to the end of the row (**4**).

On the second buttonhole row, work in rib to the bound-off stitches and then cast on the same number of stitches using either the knit-on cast-on method (see page 20) or the single cast-on method.

To work the single cast-on method, wrap the working yarn around your left thumb from front to back and secure it in your palm with your other fingers. Insert the needle upward through the strand on your thumb (**5**). Slip this loop from your thumb onto the needle, pulling the yarn to tighten it (**6**).

If using the single cast-on method, on the next row knit into the back of the cast-on stitches to tighten them (**7**).

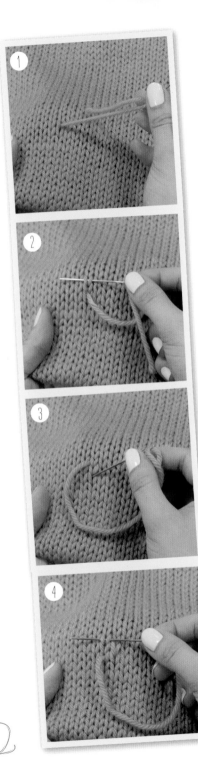

TO WET BLOCK THE PILLOW COVER

Weave in any stray yarn ends. As stockinette stitch curls at the edges, it is essential to wet block the pillow cover to the correct measurements before adding the flamingo. This helps to smooth out and set the stitches, creating a flawless fabric. Submerge the entire piece in a shallow bath of tepid water. Let it soak for a few minutes until wet through. Carefully lift it from the water supporting the entire weight, so as not to stretch it. Squeeze out excess water without wringing or twisting and place the knitting on a dry towel. Bring together the edges of the towel and press out as much moisture as possible. Now lay a clean, dry bath towel on a flat surface. Place the knitting on this towel and pin it to a width of 16" and a length of 33^1/$_2$". Leave it to dry.

TO SEW THE SIDE SEAMS

Once the work is completely dry, wrap it right side out around the pillow form with the ribbed edges overlapping. Pin the folded sides loosely to create a square, and mark where you will need to sew, ensuring the stitches line up with the corresponding row. Using mattress stitch, sew each side seam.

TO ADD THE FLAMINGO MOTIF

Make sure the button band is the correct way up before starting the color chart. The full chart is 24 sts wide and 55 sts tall. You may like to use four lengths of scrap yarn to mark the boundaries as you position it centrally on the front of the cover. Each square on the chart represents a stitch on the knitting. The flamingo is embroidered in rose, white, and black as shown on the chart.

To work the duplicate stitch, first thread the yarn onto a blunt-tipped yarn needle. Bring the yarn out, from back to front through the knitting, at the bottom of the stitch to be covered (**1**). Insert the needle at the top of the knitted stitch from right to left under the two "legs" of the knit stitch above (**2**). Reinsert the needle at the base of the stitch being covered (**3**) to complete the first duplicate stitch. Continue covering stitches along the row in the same way, working across the row from left to right (**4**).

When the embroidery is complete, sew the buttons in place and weave in any stray yarn ends.

TECHNIQUES USED

K1, p1 ribbing—see page 69
Stockinette stitch
Cast-on in middle of a row—see page 103
Wet blocking—see left
Mattress stitch—see page 49
Duplicate stitch—see left

triangle motif throw

Inspired by modern Scandinavian design, this triangle-motif throw is a stylish investment project, and a great way to hone your colorwork skills. Don't worry about trying to achieve neat sides, as the applied i-cord trim tidies up any unsightly edges.

SUPPLIES

SIZE:
Width: 43", excluding edging

Length: 52", excluding edging

YARN:
Rico *Essentials Big*

Colors: Light Gray (022), Cream (001), and Pistachio (006)

Amount: 14 x 1³⁄₄ oz (50 g) balls each of light gray and cream, and 2 balls of pistachio

KNITTING NEEDLES & EXTRAS:
Size 15 (10 mm) circular knitting needle, 40" long

Two size 15 (10 mm) double-pointed knitting needles

GAUGE:
11 sts and 14 rows to 4" measured over color patt using size 15 (10 mm) needles.

ABBREVIATIONS:
See either page 14 or the inside back-cover flap.

SPECIAL NOTE:
When working from the chart on page 108, read from right to left on knit (odd-numbered) rows and from left to right on purl (even-numbered) rows. To switch to another color, drop the working yarn and change to the second color. Strand the color not in use loosely across the wrong side of the work until needed—this creates "floats." Avoid pulling the floats too tight or the stitches will pucker at each color change. When floats span more than 5 or 6 stitches, twist the yarn not in use over the working yarn half way along the section, and continue in the current color.

TO MAKE THE THROW

Using circular needle and light gray, cast on 120 sts.

Work back and forth in rows from the color chart as follows:

Chart row 1 (RS): *K7 in light gray, k1 in cream; rep from * to end.

Chart row 2: P2 in cream, *p5 in light gray, p3 in cream; rep from * to last 6 sts, ending with p5 in light gray, p1 in cream.

The last two rows set the position of the chart.

Cont in St st working from the chart until all 8 rows of the chart have been completed.

Repeat chart rows 1–8 until your work measures 52" from cast-on edge, finishing on chart row 4 or 8. Bind off.

TO WORK THE I-CORD EDGING

Using pistachio, cast on 4 sts onto a double-pointed needle using the single of thumb cast-on method (see page 103, steps 5 and 6). Slide the 4 sts to the right end of the needle, so the working yarn is at the left, and using a second double-pointed needle, work as follows:

Row 1: Pass working yarn behind sts and pulling yarn tight on the first st, k3, sl 1, yo, pick up and knit 1 st from blanket edge (6 sts now on right needle), pass 4th and 5th sts on right needle together over 6th stitch and off right needle as if binding off (4 sts now on needle),

slide sts to the right end of needle so that working yarn is at left.

Repeat last row all around the throw until you reach first picked up stitch. Bind off.

Cut off yarn, leaving a long yarn tail. Using the yarn tail, sew the ends of the edging together with a basic whip stitch.

Weave in any stray yarn ends.

TO BLOCK THE BLANKET

To set the stitches and smooth the edges of the blanket so it lies flat, block it with a steam iron. Lay the blanket on a flat surface with a towel underneath. Hold the iron an inch above the knitting and move it slowly over a small section at a time, patting the stitches gently to encourage the process. Pay particular attention to the outside edges.

TECHNIQUES USED

Stranded colorwork
I-cord edging—see left
Whip stitch—see page 95

KEY

 Light gray—knit on a right-side row, purl on a wrong-side row

 Cream—knit on a right-side row, purl on a wrong-side row

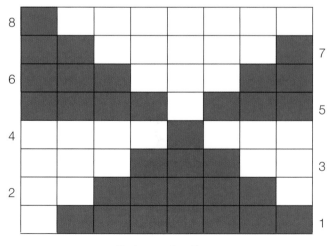

8-st repeat pattern

cotton dishcloth

Hard-wearing cotton yarn is perfect for dishcloth duties —
pretty neon cotton is even better! It's durable for scrubbing
and absorbent enough to mop up spills; just pop the cloth in
the washing machine to launder it when things get messy.
These can also be used as pot holders.

SUPPLIES

SIZE:
Width: 7"

Length: 7"

YARN:
Rico *Baby Cotton Soft DK*

Colors: Fuchsia (021) and Beige (004)

Amount: 1 x 1³/4 oz (50 g) ball of each
color

KNITTING NEEDLES & EXTRAS:
Pair of size 4 (3.5 mm) knitting needles

6" of ⁵/8"-wide cotton ribbon, for
hanging loop

Sewing needle and cotton sewing thread

GAUGE:
30 sts to 4" measured over slip-stitch
color pattern using size 4 (3.5 mm)
needles.

ABBREVIATIONS:
sl 1 with yarn in front   bring the
working yarn to the front of the
work between the two needles,
slip the next stitch purlwise (as if
to purl) and return the working
yarn to the correct position
to continue.

sl 1 with yarn in back   bring the
working yarn to the back of the
work between the two needles,
slip the next stitch purlwise (as if
to purl) and return the working
yarn to the correct position
to continue.

See also either page 14 or the inside
back-cover flap.

SPECIAL NOTE:
When changing colors between border
stitches and pattern stitches, twist the
working yarn of each color around each
other before carrying on in the alternate
color. This will avoid small holes in the
finished piece.

When changing colors between rows
allow the unused color to hang at the
side of the work and pick it up again
when you next need it.

Cut off beige and cont in fuchsia.
Work 3 rows in garter st (knit
every row).
Bind off.
Weave in any stray yarn ends.

TO BLOCK THE DISHCLOTH

Pin the dishcloth into a square
shape on an ironing board, or a
clean towel. Hold the iron just over
the surface on a steam setting,
being careful it doesn't touch your
knitting. This will set the stitches and
allow the cloth to lay flat and square.

TO FINISH

Turn under the ends of the length
of ribbon and fold the ribbon in half
widthwise. Using a sewing needle
and sewing thread, sew the hanging
loop to one corner of the dishcloth.

TO MAKE THE DISHCLOTH

Using fuchsia, cast on 54 sts.
Work 4 rows in garter stitch (knit every row).
Begin slip-stitch color pattern as follows:
Row 1: K2 in fuchsia, switch to beige, *k1, sl 1
with yarn in front; rep from * until 2 sts remain, switch
to fuchsia (use a separate small ball of fuchsia for
the 2 border sts on this side of the knitting on
rows 1 and 2), k2.
Row 2: K2 in fuchsia, switch to beige, *p1, sl 1 with yarn
in back; rep from * until 2 sts remain, switch to fuchsia,
k2.
Row 3: Using fuchsia for entire row, k2, *k1, sl 1 with
yarn in front; rep from * until 2 sts remain, k2.
Row 4: Using fuchsia for entire row, k2, *p1, sl 1 with
yarn in back; rep from * until 2 sts remain, k2.
Rows 1–4 are repeated to form the pattern.
Cont in pattern until your work measures about 6³/₄"
from cast-on edge, ending the last repeat on a row 3.

TECHNIQUES USED

Slip-stitch color pattern
Steam blocking

chevron pillow

I'm a sucker for geometric patterns and can't resist a good chevron design. This pillow cover is knitted flat in one piece. It's an opportunity to practice colorwork and to create a striking home accessory.

SUPPLIES

SIZE:
Width: 16"

Length: 16"

YARN:
Debbie Bliss *Cashmerino Aran*

Colors: Lime (502) and Ecru (101)

Amounts: 3 x 1³/₄ oz (50 g) balls in each color

KNITTING NEEDLES & EXTRAS:
Pair of size 8 (5 mm) knitting needles

Blunt-tipped yarn needle

Measuring tape

Three 1¹/₄" buttons

16" x 16" pillow form

GAUGE:
18 sts and 20 rows to 4" measured over St st using size 8 (5 mm) needles.

ABBREVIATIONS:
See either page 14 or the inside back-cover flap.

SPECIAL NOTES:
The cover is worked in stockinette stitch in colorwork using the stranding technique.

When working from the color chart on page 117, read from right to left on the knit (odd-numbered) rows and from left to right on the purl (even-numbered) rows.

To switch to another color, drop the working yarn and change to the second color. Strand the color not in use loosely across the wrong side of the work until it is needed again—this creates "floats" on the wrong side. Avoid pulling the floats too tight or the stitches will pucker at each color change.

When floats need to span more than 5 or 6 stitches, as on rows 1, 4, 5, and 8 of the chart, twist the yarn not in use over the working yarn half way along the section, and continue in the current color.

TO MAKE THE PILLOW COVER
Using lime, cast on 72 sts.

Begin k1, p1 ribbing as follows:

Rib row 1: *K1, p1; rep from * to end.

Repeat last row 8 times more. (A total of 9 rib rows have been worked.)

Begin working from color chart

Using both lime and ecru, begin working in St st from color chart on page 117 as follows:

Chart row 1 (RS): *K1 in lime, k7 in ecru; rep from * to end.

Chart row 2: P1 in lime, *p5 in ecru, p3 in lime; rep from * to last 7 sts, ending with p5 in ecru, p2 in lime.

The last two rows set the position of the chart.

Cont in St st working from the chart until all 8 rows of the chart have been completed.

Repeat chart rows 1–8 until your work measures 32" from the cast-on edge, ending with a chart row 4 or 8. (Approximately 19–20 8-row

repeats of the chart will have been worked.)

Cut off ecru and continue with lime. Knit 1 row.

Next row: *K1, p1; rep from * to end.

Work 3 rows more in k1, p1 ribbing as set, so ending with a WS row.

Buttonholes

Keeping the rib correct as set, work buttonholes over next 2 rows as follows:

Buttonhole row 1: Rib 15 sts, bind off next 4 sts, *work in rib until there are 15 sts on right needle after last bind-off, bind off next 4 sts; rep from * once more, rib to end.

Buttonhole row 2: Keeping rib correct as set, *rib 15 sts, turn work, cast on 4 sts onto the left needle using the knit-on cast-on (see page 20), turn work: rep from * twice more, rib to end.

Work 3 rows more in rib. Bind off.

TO WET BLOCK THE PILLOW COVER

Weave in any stray yarn ends.
As stockinette stitch has a tendency to curl at the edges, it is essential that you wet block the knitting to the correct measurements before sewing the side seams. This will also help to smooth out and set the stitches. Submerge the entire piece in tepid water. Let it soak for a few minutes until wet through. Then very carefully lift it from the water supporting the entire weight, so as not to stretch it.

Gently squeeze out excess water without wringing or twisting and place the knitting on a dry towel. Bring together the edges of the towel and press out as much moisture as possible.

Now lay a clean, dry bath towel on a flat surface. Place the knitting on this towel and pin it to a width of 16" and a length of 33 1/2". Leave it to dry.

TO FINISH

Once the work is completely dry, wrap it right side out around the pillow form with the ribbed edges overlapping. Pin the folded sides loosely to create a square, and mark where you will need to sew, ensuring the stitches line up with the corresponding row. Using mattress stitch, sew each side seam. Sew the buttons in place.

TECHNIQUES USED

K1, p1 ribbing—see page 69
Stranded colorwork
Cast-on in middle of a row—see page 103
Wet blocking—see page 65
Mattress stitch—see page 49

KEY

 Lime—knit on a right-side row, purl on a wrong-side row

 Ecru—knit on a right-side row, purl on a wrong-side row

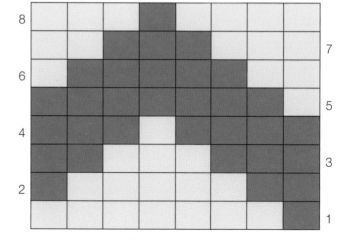

8-st repeat pattern

Egg Cozy Caps

Breakfast in bed just got a little brighter and cuter! These caps are great for using up those leftover yarns, and will keep your soft-boiled eggs warm and cozy for longer.

SIZE:
Circumference of cap: 5"

YARN:
Rico *Baby Cotton Soft DK*

Colors: Melon (020), Fuchsia (021), Lemon (028), and Mint (031)

Amount: 1/2 oz (10 g) in each color

KNITTING NEEDLES & EXTRAS:
Set of four size 5 (3.75 mm) double-pointed knitting needles

Stitch marker

3/4" pom–pom maker (or cardboard to make a template)

GAUGE:
23 sts and 29 rows to 4" measured over St st using size 5 (3.75 mm) needles.

ABBREVIATIONS:
See either page 14 or the inside back-cover flap.

TO MAKE THE CAP
Make one cap in each color.
Cast on 32 sts, using the knit cast-on method. Distribute sts on three needles (10 sts on needle one, 11 sts on needle two, 11 sts on needle three). Place a marker at beg of round and join for working in the round, being careful no sts are twisted. As this is such a small circumference, use needle three to knit the first stitch in the round 1, then change to needle four to continue.

Rounds 1, 2, 3, 4, and 5: *K1, p1; rep from * to end.
Rounds 6, 7, 8, and 9: Knit.
Round 10: [K6, k2tog] 4 times. (28 sts)
Round 11: Knit.
Round 12: [K5, k2tog] 4 times. (24 sts)
Round 13: Knit.
Round 14: [K4, k2tog] 4 times. (20 sts)
Round 15: Knit.
Round 16: [K3, k2tog] 4 times. (16 sts)

Round 17: Knit.
Round 18: [K2, k2tog] 4 times.
(12 sts)
Cut off yarn, leaving a long yarn tail. Thread the yarn tail onto a yarn needle, pass the needle through the remaining live stitches, pull to draw closed, and secure. Leave the yarn tail to use to sew the mini pom–pom to the top of the cap.

TO MAKE THE POM-POMS

Make one 1½" pom–pom in each color. If you do not have a pom–pom maker, cut two identical cardboard rings, each 2½" in diameter and with a hole in the center ¾" in diameter. Place the two rings together.

Now using the pom–pom maker or the cardboard rings, thread the yarn around and around the rings (**1**)— the more yarn you use, the thicker the pom–pom will be. Holding the wrapped rings securely, cut the yarn around the edge of the rings, inserting the scissor tip between the rings as you cut (**2** and **3**).

Tie a long length of yarn securely around the center of the strands between the rings (**4**), pull tightly and knot. Gently remove the pom–pom from the rings and fluff up the pom–pom. Trim into shape, if necessary (**5**).

Using the long yarn tail on the cap, sew the pom–pom to the center of the top of the cap.

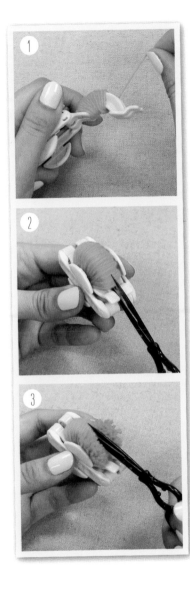

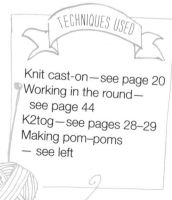

TECHNIQUES USED

Knit cast-on—see page 20
Working in the round—
see page 44
K2tog—see pages 28–29
Making pom–poms
— see left

porcupine paperweight

Meet Patrick. He's a baby porcupine. And he's ready to help you with all your desk jobs as long as they only involve sitting on your important papers all day. He loves doing this very much—almost as much as he loves the occasional cookie!

SIZE:
Width: 3¼"

Length: 5"

YARN:
Rico *Essentials Merino DK*

Colors: Rust (51), Natural (60), and Black (90)

Amounts: 1 x 1¾ oz (50 g) ball each of rust and natural, and small amount in black

KNITTING NEEDLES & EXTRAS:
Set of four size 5 (3.75 mm) double-pointed knitting needles

Polyester fiberfill (toy stuffing)

3½ oz (100 g) of small, weighted poly pellets (for toy making)

Small plastic bag to hold pellets

TECHNIQUES USED

Working in the round—see page 44

Loopy stitch—see page 124

Kfb—see pages 32–33

K2tog—see pages 28–29

Ssk—see page 14

GAUGE:
24 sts and 32 rows to 4" measured over St st using size 5 (3.75 mm) needles.

ABBREVIATIONS:
loopy stitch   See page 124.

See also either page 14 or the inside back-cover flap.

TO MAKE THE PAPERWEIGHT
Using rust, cast on 6 sts. Distribute sts evenly on three double-pointed needles (2 sts on each needle). Place a marker at beg of round and join for working in the round, being careful no stitches are twisted.

Body

Round 1: [Kfb] 6 times. (12 sts)

Round 2: Work in loopy stitch.

Round 3: [Kfb, k1] 6 times. (18 sts)

Round 4: Work in loopy stitch.

Round 5: [Kfb, k2] 6 times. (24 sts)

Round 6: Work in loopy stitch.

Round 7: [Kfb, k3] 6 times. (30 sts)

Round 8: Work in loopy stitch.

Round 9: Knit.

[Repeat rounds 8 and 9] 6 times

more, then repeat round 8 once more (11 loopy stitch rounds have been worked in total).

Now add toy stuffing to fill out the body. Place the weighted pellets in a small plastic bag and tie the bag closed. Insert the pellet bag inside the toy stuffing.

Shape face

Cut off rust and continue in natural, adding more toy stuffing as you proceed.

Round 1: K30.

Round 2: K2tog, k16, ssk, k10. (28 sts)

Round 3 and all odd rounds: Knit.

Round 4: K2tog, k14, ssk, k4, k2tog, k4. (25 sts)

Round 6: K2tog, k12, ssk, k4, k2tog, k3. (22 sts)

Round 8: K2tog, k10, ssk, k3, k2tog, k3. (19 sts)

Round 10: K2tog, k8, ssk, k3, k2tog, k2. (16 sts)

Round 12: K2tog, k6, ssk, k2, k2tog, k2. (13 sts)

Round 14: K2tog, k4, ssk, k2, k2tog, k1. (10 sts)

Round 16: K2tog, k2, ssk, k1, k2tog, k1. (7 sts)

Round 18: [K2tog] twice, k1, k2tog. (4 sts)

Cut off yarn, leaving a long tail. Thread yarn tail onto a yarn needle, pass the needle through the remaining live stitches, pull to draw closed, and secure.

TO MAKE THE EARS

There are three lines of decreases on the top of the head. Mark the ear positions on the top of the head along the top of the last loop row, 1¼" apart. Using rust and with top of head facing you, pick up and knit 3 sts at one ear position.

Row 1: P3.
Row 2: K3.
Row 3: P3.
Row 4: K3tog and fasten off.

Work another ear in the same way.

TO FINISH

Using black, embroider two little eyes and a nose as shown. Weave in any stray yarn ends.

WORKING THE LOOPY STITCH

Knit the next stitch, but don't slip it off the left needle (**1** and **2**); bring the working yarn to the front of the work between the two needles, then place the left thumb on top of the working yarn and loop the yarn around the thumb and to the back between the two needles (**3**); keeping the thumb in the loop, insert the left needle through the front loop of the stitch on the right needle and insert the right needle through the back loop of the stitch on the left needle, and knit these 2 stitches together (**4** and **5**). Repeat in each stitch to the end of the round. Work a loopy stitch round and a knit round alternately to form the pattern.

choosing yarns

The yarns used for the projects in this book are listed here, with their specifications. It is always best to use the yarn recommended in the knitting pattern in order to achieve the result shown. If you decide to use a substitute yarn, find one that is similar in weight (see pages 12–13), texture, and fiber content. To determine the weight (thickness) of a yarn, take into account the generic description of the weight and the manufacturer's recommended gauge.

Be sure to calculate the amount of substitute yarn you will need by yards (meters) per ball, not by ounces (grams).

Debbie Bliss Cashmerino Aran
An Aran-weight yarn; 55% extra-fine merino wool, 35% microfiber, 12% cashmere; 98 yd (90 m) per 1$\frac{3}{4}$ oz (50 g) ball; recommended gauge—18 sts and 24 rows to 4" over St st using US size 8 (5 mm) needles.

Debbie Bliss Luxury Donegal Tweed Chunky
A bulky-weight yarn; 90% merino wool, 10% angora; 109 yd (100 m) per 3$\frac{1}{2}$ oz (100 g) ball; recommended gauge—12 sts and 19 rows to 4" over St st using US size 10$\frac{1}{2}$ (6.5 mm) needles.

Debbie Bliss Rialto Chunky
A bulky-weight yarn; 100% merino wool; 66 yd (60 m) per 1$\frac{3}{4}$ oz (50 g) ball; recommended gauge—15 sts and 21 rows to 4" over St st using US size 10$\frac{1}{2}$ (6.5 mm) needles.

Erika Knight Blue Wool
A double-knitting-weight wool yarn; 100% wool; 60 yd (55 m) per $\frac{7}{8}$ oz (25 g) ball; recommended gauge—22 sts and 30 rows to 4" over St st using US size 6 (4 mm) needles.

Erika Knight Maxi Wool
A super-bulky yarn; 100% wool; 87 yd (80 m) per 3$\frac{1}{2}$ oz (100 g) ball; recommended gauge—8 sts and 12 rows to 4" over St st using US size 17 (12 mm) needles.

Erika Knight Vintage Wool
An Aran-weight wool yarn; 100% wool; 95 yd (8 m) per 1$\frac{3}{4}$ oz (50 g) ball; recommended gauge—18 sts and 24 rows to 4" over St st using US size 8 (5 mm) needles.

King Cole Bamboo Cotton DK
A double-knitting-weight yarn; 50% bamboo, 50% cotton; 251 yd (230 m) per 3$\frac{1}{2}$ oz (100 g) ball; recommended gauge—22 sts and 30 rows to 4" over St st using US size 6 (4 mm) needles.

Rico Creative Twist Super Chunky
A super-bulky-weight yarn; 80% acrylic, 20% alpaca; 82 yd (75 m) per 3$\frac{1}{2}$ oz (100 g) ball; recommended gauge—9 sts and 12 rows to 4" over St st using US size 15 (10 mm) needles.

Rico Essentials Big
A bulky-weight yarn; 50% wool, 50% acrylic; 52 yd (48 m) per 1$\frac{3}{4}$ oz (50 g) ball; recommended gauge—11 sts and 16 rows to 4" over St st using US sizes 10$\frac{1}{2}$–11 (7–8 mm) needles.

Rico Baby Cotton Soft DK
A double-knitting-weight yarn; 50% cotton, 50% acrylic; 136 yd (125 m) per 1$\frac{3}{4}$ oz (50 g) ball; recommended gauge—22 sts and 28 rows to 4" over St st using US size 4 (3.5 mm) needles.

Rico Essentials Merino DK
A double-knitting-weight yarn; 100% wool; 131 yd (120 m) per 1$\frac{3}{4}$ oz (50 g) ball; recommended gauge—22 sts and 28 rows to 4" over St st using US size 6 (4 mm) needles.

Rico Essentials Soft Merino Aran
An Aran-weight yarn; 100% merino wool; 109 yd (100 m) per 1$\frac{3}{4}$ oz (50 g) ball; recommended gauge—18 sts and 24 rows to 4" over St st using US size 8 (5 mm) needles.

Rowan Wool Cotton DK
A double-knitting-weight yarn; 50% cotton, 50% merino wool; 123 yd (113 m) per 1$\frac{3}{4}$ oz (50 g) ball; recommended gauge—22–24 sts and 30–32 rows to 4" over St st using US sizes 5–6 (3.75–4 mm) needles.

Sirdar Flirt DK
A double-knitting-weight wool yarn; 80% bamboo sourced viscose, 20% wool; 104 yd (95 m) per 1$\frac{3}{4}$ oz (50 g) ball; recommended gauge—22 sts and 28 rows to 4" over St st using US size 6 (4 mm) needles.

Sirdar Snuggly Baby Bamboo DK
Same description and specifications as Sirdar *Flirt DK.*

index

THANK YOU THANK YOU THANK YOU

A very big thank you to Lisa at Quadrille for giving me the opportunity to write this book; and to Christine, Keiko, Gemma, and Chinh for all their hard work making it happen — a wonderful team to work with!

To Ben for buying me my very first knitting book, and for always being there to listen to my ideas, offer constructive opinions, and keep me motivated along the way.

To my family — Mum, Dad and Alsie for their unwavering support and encouragement.

Thank you also to Debbie Bliss, Erika Knight, and Rico for providing yarn for the majority of the projects.

Publishing Director Jane O'Shea
Commissioning Editor Lisa Pendreigh
Editor Sally Harding
Creative Director Helen Lewis
Art Direction & Design Claire Peters
Designer Gemma Hogan
Photographer Keiko Oikawa
Stylist and Illustrator Christine Leech
Production Director Vincent Smith
Production Controller Aysun Hughes

Quadrille *craft*

www.quadrillecraft.com

First edition for North America published in 2015 by Barron's Educational Series, Inc.

First published in 2014 by Quadrille Publishing Ltd.
www.quadrille.co.uk

Text, projects, designs, artwork & illustrations
© 2014 Jessica Biscoe
Photography © 2014 Keiko Oikawa
Illustrations © 2014 Christine Leech
Design & layout © 2014 Quadrille Publishing Ltd.

All inquiries should be addressed to:
Barron's Educational Series, Inc.
250 Wireless Boulevard
Hauppauge, NY 11788
www.barronseduc.com

ISBN: 978-1-4380-0597-3

Library of Congress Control No.: 2014951247

Printed in China

9 8 7 6 5 4 3 2 1